A Rose in a Ditch

...ing

Ra... ...earl S. Buck's daughter

My friend, Heather Doherty, surprised me several years ago with a painting of a blooming rose in a ditch after she heard my story. This painting has been hanging in our sitting room since that day.

A Rose in a Ditch

by

Julie Henning

Raised as Pearl S. Buck's daughter

WCP

Pearl S. Buck Writing Center Press
Perkasie, Pennsylvania

ISBN-13: 9781704786438

First Edition

Published by
WCP
Pearl S. Buck Writing Center Press
520 Dublin Road
Perkasie, PA 18944
www.psbi.org/writingcenter

Dedication

With love, I dedicate this book to my three Mothers.

Umma
Jung Song Ja

Mother Pearl
Pearl S. Buck

"Umma"
Jean Price

Standing:
Jean and Harry Price
Seated:
Diane Bishop, Douglas,
Julie and Doug Henning

Helen Henning was an unselfish mother-in-law to me.

Acknowledgements

I would like to acknowledge the following people, without whom this book would never have been written.

Carol Wedeven is a gifted, precise, creative author. Over the past several years, she always seemed to know the exact question to ask me at the precise, God-ordained time to cause me to reflect upon events and people in my life that resulted in the content of this book.

Many thanks to Cindy Louden, Anne Kaler, Linda Donaldson, and Eileen Yevcak from the Pearl S. Buck Writing Center, who eagerly, carefully, and lovingly helped with the editing of this Amerasian's writing!

Some friends and sisters-of-my-heart, shared encouraging words, phone calls, texts, and hugs when they were sorely needed. Lynn, Darla, Mary Pat, Heather, Cheryl, Pat, Jerie, Marianne, Dorothy, Terre, Diane, Lydia, Barb, and Joyce kept me smiling as I wrote.

My friend, Heather Doherty, surprised me several years ago with a painting of a single blooming rose after she heard my story. This painting has been hanging in our sitting room since the day she presented it to me. God used Heather to have the cover picture ready long before this book was conceived.

My sons, my daughters-in-love, and five precious grandsons are gifts from God who daily bring pleasure, pride, and much purpose to my life. Doug, Kandece, Tre, Cole, Cade; and, Pete, Renee, Carter, and Mason: You are the bestest of the bestest (Mom-mom can get away with her own version of Korean-English). I was born with just one person on earth who cared about me and for me. Now, you fill my life with love and joy. I am truly blessed!

Doug, God has made you to be my rock. My ups and downs and insecurities required a steady, godly, servant/leader like you. God brought you into my life at just the right time. He used you to bring me to Jesus, and spending life with you has been pure joy. I love who I am when I am with you. Your patience in typing this manuscript, with just enough revisions and edits to make it readable while keeping it in my voice, is remarkable. I love you.

From God and through him and to him are all things. To him be glory forever. – Romans 11:36

Table of Contents

Chapter One

My Umma

I was born a child of a Korean mother and an American GI near the end of the Korean War. That simple fact has, in many ways, shaped my story.

My Korean mother, Umma, grew up on her father's farm in North Korea. In her childhood, Umma was often hungry. She was living with her ten siblings. Rice and vegetables were scarce. The North Korean Communist leader Kim Il-Sung, with the help from the Soviet Union and Kim's guerilla fighters, moved into her countryside. They pillaged the already meager food supply. While Umma loved living with her parents, brothers, and sisters, facing starvation became real. As a late teenager, Umma lost all hope of ever living a good life in her homeland. She knew what she had to do. "Our large family did not have enough food," she said. "I was afraid for all of us. I thought that if I left, there would be one less mouth to feed." I often wondered how my mom could leave her family behind?

My Umma was born during the thirty-six years of Japanese colonial rule of Korea which ended when World War II concluded in 1945. During the Japanese occupation, Koreans were not allowed to speak the Korean language in school and in public places. The Japanese burned Korean history books and forced Umma's people to worship Shintoism, the religion of Japan. Japan attempted to destroy the Korean culture and the spirit of its people. But the resilient Koreans persisted until World War II ended and Japanese rule was terminated. Korea was then divided into North and South. The Soviet Union had been given North Korea, while the Americans assisted South Korea.

Hunger and the thought of communist rule drove Umma from her family – the only security she had ever known. She prayed to Buddha for protection from harm during her scary, lonely escape. I often wondered if she crawled through tunnels or if she cut herself on the many barbed-wire fences along the way. What did she do for food? How terrified she must have been! Umma spoke little of these times. Perhaps this part of her life was so deep that her heart would have burst if she dared utter a word about her journey into South Korea. She never heard anything about the rest of her family. I do not know anything about my grandparents or uncles and aunts. I hope my Umma's family did not starve!

When Umma came to South Korea, she met a very kind man who wanted to marry her. Not long after their marriage, he joined the South Korean army at the start of the Korean War. Shortly after he left for the war, Umma had a baby daughter, my half-sister. Umma prayed to Buddha for her husband's protection in hope of the day he would return to hold his daughter. But, Umma's fears became her reality. The husband she loved was killed during the war. Fear and loneliness again overwhelmed her. She was faced with raising a daughter alone. Umma told me years later, "I had a daughter, your half-sister. I did everything I could for her, but I had no husband and no money. My greatest fear was that she would starve like many other hungry children at that time."

Umma often harvested free wild vegetables growing wherever farmers had not planted rice or near the mountain's edge. During the growing season, she would also purchase the farmer's vegetables and sell them from house to house for a small profit. Her basket filled with sesame leaves, bean sprouts, sweet potatoes, and scallions was carried on her head as she sold her produce each day.

But, what did my mother do in her most desperate times? Was she forced to steal? I remember once when I was a child, I was so hungry, I broke God's rule and stole a sweet potato from someone's farm. I thought God would surely understand why I did it. But I still felt guilty. Did Umma steal? Did she feel guilty about it? Some of the farmers were kind to Umma, but times were difficult for everyone. She may have had to do more than beg!

When Korean women got married, they lived with their husband's family and the new couple took care of his parents. It was their duty.

This was an ancient Confucian value. But where were my paternal grandparents through this time? Did they abandon my mother and half-sister after their son was killed in battle? Or, were they killed in the war, too?

As the war continued, food became even more scarce. My half-sister had almost nothing to eat. She was always hungry. They also had no indoor toilet. My mother told me that she kept a little urn by the bed so she could relieve herself at night. She would then empty it in the morning by the ditch outside. One day, my sister drank the tepid liquid before Umma could empty it. "That's how hungry your sister was," she said. After a brief lifetime of hunger, my sister grew pale and thin. Besides praying to Buddha for food, my mother had exhausted all other resources for feeding her daughter. My half-sister cried out in weak despair. Before her second birthday, my half-sister – whose name Umma never told me – died in my mother's arms. How cruel war can be! We rarely talked of her. I do not know how or where she was buried.

Umma wrapped all her earthly belongings – a cup, bowl, chop sticks, spoons, a pot, and a cutting knife – into a scarf that had belonged to her mother, my grandmother. She balanced all of this on her head and headed south from Seoul to find safety. Most South Koreans fled Seoul in 1950-51 to escape the North Korean and Chinese armies that came over the border like a swarm of ants. The American army and South Korean soldiers retreated from the sheer manpower of the communist armies. In the grueling heat of a Korean summer, my mother, and thousands of other refugees, headed South for safety. This painful journey has been documented in Korean history books. It was a walk of both fear and courage. It was a walk to avoid the pursuing North Korean army. It was a walk to survive.

My mother's white dress was tied around her waist and surely was covered in grime as she walked and walked on the dirt road, passing streams and rice paddies. Others were pushing carts or were walking beside carts pulled by oxen. Older sisters cared for younger sisters, while the sons pushed the carts carrying the weak and elderly. Injured people, wrapped in bandages, limped along with wooden sticks. All walked as fast as their feet could carry them. What compelled them to march on? What did they feel? Again, Umma shared little of this journey. The pain was just too great.

The refugees crowded into the southern tip of the Korean peninsula – the city of Pusan. By that time, General MacArthur had stemmed the southern surge of the North Korean and Chinese armies. In Pusan, frightened hungry children cried weakly – a sound my mother remembered all too well. My mother was a widow in Pusan, without much education or means to earn a living. "I needed money to buy food," Umma told me, "so I started working at an American G.I. coffeehouse. One day I met a kind American soldier, known by his friends as 'Shorty.'" He and my mother became very close. They found comfort in each other in a war-torn wasteland. What goes through the mind and heart of a man and woman during the horrors of war? Was the moment of time all they had since there was no certainty of tomorrow?

I was born on May 14, 1953. My mother and father called me 'Julie.' That's what I was told. Julie – the name my father gave me. When I was less than three months old, the Korean 'Conflict' ended. On July 27, 1953, an armistice between North and South Korea was signed. It would have been wonderful if my father could have stayed in Korea, but his tour of duty ended when I was about one-year-old and he returned to America. My mother told me he was a kind man and very good to her. She loved him very much. She said, "One of my happiest times of life was when Shorty and I were with our wonderful daughter." Umma told me that Shorty wanted to take me with him to America, but I am thankful that my mom didn't consent to his wishes. According to Umma, he said he was married and had three children in the States. How would I have been received by them? I doubt his family ever knew anything of us.

Did my father really love me as Umma said? I would like to think that my father wanted me, but I am not sure. Maybe it was just a story that my mom made up to protect my feelings.

After my father left, my mother decided that if I were going to survive in a society which rejected mixed-blood children, now called Amerasians, I needed to be like other Korean children. My mother changed my name to 'Sooni.' "You are sweet. Your name will be Sooni."

I later learned that I was born when my mother was twenty-three. She was born in September, 1930. Her parents named her Jung Song Ja. She was a blood member of a family which made her a Korean citizen.

She had a family name, and according to the law of the land, she 'existed.' But, when I was born, things were very different. Since my mother was Korean and my father an American G.I., I was not a full-blooded Korean. This was an unspeakable cultural taboo in 1950s South Korea.

The Korean government did not recognize my birth. I did not have a last name, a birth certificate, or citizenship. According to Korean law at the time, a child is the citizen of his father's country. So, the Koreans considered me to be an American. But, according to American law, a child is a citizen of his birth country. So, my father's country would consider my birth country to be Korea!

I grew up thinking that neither country wanted me. I once thought that I belonged somewhere in the middle of the Pacific Ocean – between the two countries of my parents' birth. I knew I existed, but I was a child without a homeland. I had no family name, no country, and I didn't look like the other Korean children!

Amerasians came onto the scene after World War II and the Korean War. We were caught between two extreme cultures. In the 50s and 60s, this new half-breed was despised, ridiculed, and discriminated against by my motherland. Koreans are very proud of their pure race and orderly nation. Consequently, these fatherless, nameless, impoverished Amerasians were often aborted or left on the streets to die unless some kind heart would come and care for them. A mother who bore a half-breed was a marked woman, unemployable. Of course, no Korean man in his right mind would marry a woman who had defiled herself with a white foreigner. It was like the scarlet letter 'A' was on my mother's chest.

My mother chose to keep me! She could have chosen the way of many others at the time. But, she lived with alienation to keep her Amerasian daughter, who would herself grow up in a society that rejected her. Life was hard after the war, but especially for the mixed-race children and their mothers. But Umma chose me and chose life – for me, for herself, and for us! Umma needed to find a means to support us. To stay alive, we moved north to the military village of Pubwon-ni, near the Demilitarized Zone (DMZ, or 38th Parallel) where many American military bases were located.

Seeing the G.Is. made me wish my father was with us. I didn't even know what he looked like. When I was at an age of understanding,

I would inquire of Umma to find out more about my father. Umma would just hold me tightly in response and cry. I would stop asking – for that day at least. I do remember she told me that Shorty was an Army cook and a lieutenant. That's about all I remember of what I was told.

I don't blame my father for leaving us. I understand the choices he had to make. He was an American G.I. halfway around the world, away from his family. He had lonely moments. He was comforted by Umma. She, too, was lonely and scared after losing her husband and daughter. Some could say they were wrong for living together outside of marriage. I didn't ask to be the product of such circumstances, but there I was with a wrong face at the wrong time.

Chapter Two

Hunger & The Alley

Umma gave me everything she had. She seemed to not need much for herself – except for me – her only daughter. I did not know what I did not have. I was content in my mother's presence, provision, and love. When we were hungry, Umma and I often went to the mountains to find free vegetables. She always seemed to know what types of vegetables and mushrooms to pick. There were so many different colors and shapes of mushrooms. But we often had no rice. We were hungry today. We hoped a G.I. friend would come. When they came, we had money to buy rice. The Korean government did not have any means to assist poor people. What little we had is what we ate! I prayed to the gods of Buddha that more G.I. friends would come.

The hot, humid summer days seemed to make my face drip. My stomach was growling and it hurt. I was hungry – very hungry. All I could think about was when I could eat again. I hugged myself and tried and tried to rub the hunger away. I pumped some water by the well and drank as much as I could. For a moment, I was relieved from my hunger. But that feeling did not last. Umma had no money in her draw-string purse. She had no food. I wanted to be brave for my mom. I cried silently in my heart. Am I going to starve today? Is this how my sister felt before she died?

Hunger came to visit so often. It kept eating at my belly. The only thing I could think about was food. "Umma, will we eat today?" Umma's eyes answered me – often they said, "No." Umma had to pay Mamason the rent for our one room house and there had been no food since Tuesday. Umma's hot water would not fill my belly. I thought about food even more when I told myself not to think about it. I wished the night to come soon so I could sleep and forget. By the third day, I wasn't as hungry as the first two days. I just felt tired and weak.

"Will a G.I. friend come tonight, Umma?" It's Friday. G.I.'s usually come on Friday and Saturday nights.

Umma and I washed a day's dust from our bodies and cleansed our teeth with salt on our second finger. We did not have toothbrushes or toothpaste. We found nothing free to eat in the fields today, not even by the edge of the mountains. Other hungry people had discovered anything edible before we arrived. "Time to sleep," Umma said while putting an arm around me. "Even the moon is saying, 'Good night, Soonyia.'"

Umma unfolded our table and pushed it to the corner of our small room we called home. She placed comforters over it and made a nice cozy tent for me. I enjoyed living under the make-believe tent. We talked under the tent. "Oh, Sweetie, I have a dream. In my dream, you will grow to be big and strong and get an education. You will go to school, Soonyia."

Umma put her fingers through my hair and kissed my cheek and told me that I must not make any noise and be very quiet if a G.I. friend came. "But I don't have to be quiet when Aunties come," I said.

"When Auntie Sughil comes, she wants to talk to both of us. But when a G.I. comes, he wants only to talk to me." I did not understand all of her words, but I knew when it was time to stop asking questions. I lay still as a dead grasshopper as someone knocked on the door. I could hear our door slide open followed by a G.I.'s voice. Umma and her visitor were talking and then I heard his boots clunk to the floor with laughter and other noises came from both of them. Soon after, the rice door opened and closed. He was gone.

"Are you asleep, Soonyia?" "No, Umma." Umma removed the comforter and touched my face. "You are getting so big! From now on, you are big enough to play outside when a G.I. friend comes.

I am getting big. That means I can go to school soon. And, tomorrow we can eat!

When G.I.'s came to our one-room home, I had no place to go. I played outside by the edge of the alley. The alley was about twenty-five feet long and five feet wide. A very high wall from the drug store was on one side. It was often dark, but it was my alley. I knew it well. When I was younger, I thought the alley was so big. When it would rain, I had to step side-to-side at the edges of the alley so I would not get wet by the puddle in the middle. I felt safe in the alley because I could see a flickering candlelight or an oil lamp through our rice paper door. I sat on the bare ground and drew in the dirt with my sticks to occupy time. Time went faster when I spent it drawing. I drew our outside shelf – a strong shelf under the edge of our roof. My mom and I would step on that shelf to go in and out of our house. But when my mom was cooking, she would wipe it and use it as a counter top to prepare our food.

When Umma cooked outside, I watched with curiosity. As much as I wanted to help, she often responded, "You are my princess. You don't have to work." I probably watched her more because I was not allowed to help! There were times when the rain would extinguish the coals and Umma would have to rekindle the fire to finish preparing our daily meal.

On the ground, I also drew our old water pump. It was surrounded by many flat stones near our door. I could picture my mom talking to my Aunties by the pump while they were 'scrubbing' the brown rice against the large stone with smaller stones to make the rice whiter. I loved seeing my mom with all the Aunties. They were the only friends my mother had. Wealthier people ate white rice and poorer people ate brown rice. Later on, I found out that the brown rice we poor people ate was actually more nutritious than the white rice desired by the wealthy. After drawing the water pump and thinking about all that happened around the well, I stopped to take a drink from the well. I pumped and pumped and added some water to start the pump working. When the water finally poured out, I sipped water in my cupped hands. I loved the cold water splashing on my face. And water made my tummy full a little longer.

My next piece of alley "artwork" was Umma's rice container. This was the aluminum container with flowers etched on the lid. My father gave that to my mom before he went back to America. It was my mom's prized possession. Next to my figure, I drew Umma with a large heart on her chest. I wish I could draw other children, but I was the only child among all the Aunties living nearby. I wanted other children to play with me. But for now, the alley was like my living room, play room, and playground...my own little world. My stick, many pebbles and stones gathered by the creek, and pots and pans made from clay that we scraped from the creek's bottom, were my toys. I spent hours at a time playing kitchen with them.

It was easy to draw clay pots. Umma stored her kimchee in clay pots resembling what I drew. When October came, Umma would save up as much money as she could and buy a big box of Napa cabbage. Then she would sprinkle coarse sea salt to marinate. Next, she would mix shredded moo radish, scallions, red chili pepper flakes, salted shrimp, garlic and ginger. She would carefully insert all these seasonings between the layers of cabbage. When it was all finished, the kimchee would go into a big clay pot and we would bury it under the ground having only the lid of the pot above the soil. Umma told me that this was the way we could enjoy kimchee during the winter season. I could eat it morning, noon, and night! Thinking about food while drawing in the alley made me even more hungry!

While in the alley, I stood up and gathered many stones that were in the corner. My mom and I found these stones by our creek. I had more than one hundred stones. I would invent games where I would count and recount the stones as I tossed them in the air and caught them before they hit the ground.

On Fridays and Saturdays, I spent more time in the alley with my drawings, stone games, and clay dishes. When it was too cold, or wet for me to be outside, my mom asked a lady down the street to watch over me at her house. My mom washed her clothes to thank her.

When one of Umma's G.I. friends left, she came out and said, "Soonyia, I have a surprise for you." She looked at the drawings, smiled and said, "You draw well, Soonyia!" I loved seeing her smile. Her eyes twinkled like a starry night sky. Umma grabbed my hand tightly and hurriedly crossed the street to the Chinese restaurant. An army jeep roared past creating dust clouds from our dirt road. Sometimes a water wagon would spray the road to settle the dust, but that never lasted long. Umma ordered my favorite veal with shredded lettuce. We sat waiting until the food was prepared. It seemed like an eternity. Umma gave the clerk some won. She then put some soy sauce on the shredded lettuce. Umma said, "Come, my princess. Let us go home now and eat." We crossed the street carefully carrying the veal and the lettuce, but at the same time hurrying to get home to eat! Once I sat, my legs crossed on the floor under our low table, Mom put our much-anticipated meal in front of me. I wanted to eat so fast, but Umma again reminded me to chew my food thirty times before I swallow. Did she tell me that because my stomach was empty for a long time? It was hard to chew for that long. The food seemed to disappear in my mouth.

"Where is your food?" I asked Umma. "I will eat it later," she answered with a smile. She watched as I ate. Soy sauce made the crunchy lettuce even more tasty. I was getting better at using chopsticks. My mom would cut the meat in small pieces with her kitchen knife. I think my stomach was surprised to have meat. Meat was expensive and we ate it no more than a handful of time in a year. Umma didn't buy any food for herself from the restaurant that night. She wanted me to eat as much as I could, then she would eat the leftovers. I left food on the plate so she could have some, too. Today was a special treat. She watched me eat with a big smile on her face. I smiled back. Her contentment was so good to see.

The only predictable time each year that we would eat beef was on New Year's Day. My mom would save money for many days to buy beef and long rice cakes to make duk gook, a traditional New Year's Day soup. That is when I would get to taste meat in soup broth. The meal on New Year's Day was an extra treat. Again, my mom just watched me eat with a contented smile on her face. We were together and our bellies were full. That makes a special day!

New Year's Day in Korea is a grand holiday. On that day, I became one year older. Everyone in Korea celebrated their birthday on New Year's Day! In addition, all Koreans are one-year-old when they are born. The gestation period is counted as one year of life. For example, a person born in December is one-year-old at birth. Then, when January arrives, that person becomes two!

Koreans look at aging differently than in the West. They enjoy becoming older because being older means you are more respected.

So, on New Year's Day, Umma and I knew it was important to visit the Aunties at Mamason's house which was behind our house. In the farm village, we would also greet Halmauni. These are all people that I respected greatly because of their age. Of course, they were good to me also! I bowed all the way down to the floor and wished them health and wealth for the New Year. Then they would give me a small present and perhaps even some won. One year, my mom was able to purchase a hanbok, a beautiful Korean ceremonial dress. She was so proud to be able to give it to me. I never wanted to take it off! I danced and swirled around the room while my mom watched me with the biggest smile. All was well in our world. Just Umma and me.

I was Umma's life. Her purpose was to do whatever she could do to keep me alive. She was not going to lose another daughter. She knew that the only way for me to get out of my impoverished predicament was to get an education. After the Korean War, the goal of many Korean women was to get their Amerasian children adopted by an American family and get an education. My Mom heard many wonderful stories about America from the G.I.'s she knew and that is where she wanted me to be. Though we were so poor, it was the only life I knew. I was so thankful to be my mother's daughter. She loved me with all of her heart. Love eased our difficult living conditions. The Aunties called me "a rose in a ditch." Perhaps they hoped that I might overcome my circumstances. Umma showed me how meaningful and honorable it was to be a mother. Her constant love, affection, encouragement, and care made my heart full despite my empty stomach. My mom could give me the best hugs, kisses, and piggy back rides, turning and twirling me in our one room house. Our giggles filled the room.

Chapter Three

Pubwon-Ni

My Mom and I lived in Pubwon-ni, a small town very close to the Demilitarized Zone. We were close enough to North Korea that on some mornings, we could even hear North Koreans shouting propaganda to us through megaphones. We would hear how great their life was, but the story I heard in school was very different. We were poor. The North Koreans were even more destitute. Our one-room house had no running water, no electricity, an outhouse, and an outside kitchen that was only covered by the edge of the roof. Quite often, my mom would get wet as she prepared our food. She told me how she found this house. The morning after a house fire where we had previously lived when I was very young, my mom tied me on her back with her scarf and went to a coffee house on Reservoir Road. Umma found a Korean woman dressed in western clothes standing outside the door. Umma asked her where we could find a house and a wet nurse for me. She told Umma to go north towards the village of Munsan-ni to find a woman on her farm with a son and pigs!

In Korea, elderly women were called 'halmauni.' My halmauni helped to nurse other women's babies. My mother's milk had run dry. When Umma asked this lady, she said it was her honor to nurse me. My mom was so thankful she was able to find a lady to feed me milk. The money from my father was dwindling, and my mother shared these concerns with my wet nurse. The kind lady told her, "Mamasan has a back room. Perhaps you could rent it." My mom was so thankful. She had found a house to live in and a wet nurse to feed me. Our house was behind the drug store where two busy streets crossed. The G.I.'s called this intersection "Mickey Mouse Corner." Day and night jeeps, army trucks, and busses created lots of dust as they roared by the Chinese restaurant, dress shops, the bakery, the butcher shop, and street vendors selling vegetables, rice, and fruits. Some hungry children in rags roamed the streets hoping to find something to trade for food to fill their hungry bellies. War created hunger, poverty, orphans, wives without husbands, and mixed-race children like me. My mom and I often looked for free food. My Umma was so good pulling different greens. She could get the roots and all. After washing them clean, she would steam them and season with sesame oil, soy sauce, and hot pepper. My mom was so good at preparing all kinds of mushrooms, too. Some days we would spend hours collecting snails from the creek. My Mom would boil them and we would use soft pins to pull the meat out of the shell.

I was a master at catching grasshoppers. Grasshoppers are sleepier in the morning, so I would go to a rice paddy soon after waking up. Farmers did not mind me coming. They knew I would be very careful between the rows of rice reeds. When I carefully parted the reeds, I could see young, tender, plump, green grasshoppers holding on the reed. I would snatch one up! Then, I would bend the back of the grasshopper's neck which would make somewhat of a loop. I would pull another rice reed and string it through that loop much like one would string popcorn through a needle and thread. When I had strung two or three long reeds of grasshoppers, my morning work was successful. When I returned home, I would be greeted by mom's smile. She would unstring all the grasshoppers into her large pot while keeping the lid open just enough to fit the grasshoppers in while not letting them escape. Next, she would quickly close the lid of the pot and put it on the coals. As the pot heated up, strange noises came from inside the pot. When the noise subsided, we then opened the lid. All the grasshoppers were roasted nice and golden brown. My Mom would sprinkle some salt on them, we would take off the wings and legs since they were too prickly to eat. Mom and I would giggle together as we ate our captured protein with delight.

During the weekend evenings, Mamasan's coffee house customers sang loud Korean songs and tapped chopsticks at the edge of the table as they dined next to our wall. The loud talking, singing, and laughter lasted most of the night. I lay next to Umma, holding onto her and trying to sleep. Sleep usually did not come too quickly amidst all that noise.

Umma pulled more comforters over me to muffle the noise. "When can we go see Halmauni?" I asked Umma. "We can go see her tomorrow!" I liked going to see Halmauni and her pigs. Halmauni was my wet nurse when I was little. But she was more than that to me. She was like a grandmother to me. If my real grandmothers were alive, they would be living in faraway places like North Korea or America.

Halmauani's pigs loved food scraps just like pigs should! After the loud nights at Mamasan's, there was always food left all over the floor and tables. Since Mamasan didn't have any animals, she allowed me to take the party scraps to Halmauni's pigs. I closed my eyes and could picture the pigs enjoying all the scraps. They looked forward to me coming. I wanted this night to go fast. But the loud noise at Mamasan's coffee house persisted. Sleep just did not come.

I lifted the comforters and peeked at the moon through the open window. Could my father see the same moon in America? Umma told me how he loved holding me, tickling me, and singing to me. But I did not remember any of this. I did not even know how he looked. Did his eyes twinkle when he saw me? Did I bring a wide smile to his face?

I was glad to hear the rooster crow. This morning we get to go to see Halmauni and take the food scraps to the pigs! I didn't hear any sound from Mamason's house. The Aunties might still be asleep. I do not know when they went to bed, but it certainly was after I fell asleep. I ran to our pump and splashed water on my face. Umma handed me some salt. I dabbed my second finger with salt and rubbed against my teeth extra hard this morning to make them even more clean. I ran my wet hands to smooth my wrinkled clothes.

"Soonyia, breakfast is ready!" Umma boiled left-over rice from yesterday with a lot of water. The rice becomes much bigger when boiled a second time and the consistency becomes thicker. I loved the warmth and how it made my tummy feel full. As Umma washed the bowls, pots, and spoons, I quietly walked over to Mamasan's door and grabbed the pigs' bucket which had a good amount of scraps that the Aunties had cleaned off the tables and floors from last evening's customers. Finally, Umma and I were ready.

At the end of our alley, we turned right onto Main Street. Some people were riding bicycles with baskets on their backs and some were pushing a cart full of vegetables. A jeep roared by kicking up a lot of dust from the dirt road. We passed the clinic where Umma had to go to have her health checked. Umma said she needed a doctor's note to have G.I. friends come to visit her. I enjoyed carrying the bucket. It made me feel big. But pretty soon Umma carried it while holding my hand. It was a long walk to Halmauni's house, but I enjoyed looking at the farm houses built with mud and straw. The different rice paddies and vegetable gardens helped make the walk seem to go faster. Umma pointed to the porch of one of the houses. Beneath the straw roof hung a string of red peppers. "See the red peppers?" Umma called out. "A baby boy must have been born at that house." I asked Umma what was hung outside her house when I was born. She told me that since she did not have a porch, they could not hang anything out to announce my birth. "Your father and I were just happy to have you!" But normally, white pieces of paper and charcoal are displayed for a baby girl's birth.

I wanted to see Halmauni's house the most. I so hoped Halmauni would make us turnip soup. It was the best! "I see Halmauni!" I screamed. I let go of Umma's hand, ran to her and wrapped my entire self around her waist. She hugged me with a great big hug and a smile to match. She told me how pleased she was to see me and how big I was growing. I glanced around and heard one of the pigs screech, "Oink!" Halmauni laughed. "She wants to see you. She's been waiting for you." After I poured the food in the pig's feeding trough, I stood on the bottom rung of the fence watching each of the pigs push its face into the food scraps thoroughly enjoying a treat.

Umma opened our rice paper covered door and stepped out to the alley and said, "Sooynia, let's go pick dandelions today for supper." I always loved when we could go to the fields together. We walked through our alley and turned onto Main Street. We passed the drug store on Mickey Mouse corner and headed north on Reservoir Road on the outskirts of Pubwon-ni. We were then able to find free vegetables after passing rice paddies and vegetable gardens.

My Mom was so good at pulling the entire dandelion, roots and all. I was an expert at just pulling the leaves! Then she would have to pull and twist until the entire plant came out. One by one, we put the dandelions on Umma's ever-present scarf. Umma shared with me how she and her sisters would pick dandelions in North Korea. I asked Umma why she had left her family. She told me that life there was so difficult. Her entire family was always hungry. If she left them, there would be more food for the rest of the family.

"Look, Soonyia!" Umma pointed to a field covered with crimson clovers. We picked the stems as low as we could go, and my mother braided a chain of clovers long enough to put it on my hair, then braided my hair around the clover to tighten the edge. She also made a clover ring for my finger. "You are a princess!" I touched the fuzzy flowers on my head and felt very special and pretty. "I am a princess and you are my Queen. I love you, Umma!"

Inside our one-room house, our space was big enough for living or sleeping, but not at the same time. When we ate, we would unfold our low table, cross our legs under it and sit on the floor. After eating, we would fold the table and lean it against one side of the wall. When it was time to sleep, we unfolded comforters and placed them on the floor. Instantly, our home became our bedroom. I wrapped myself around my Mom's arm and snuggled up to her. My mom held me tight and said, "Soonyia, tomorrow is going to be a special day. After you wash well, I want you to put on a new dress." I asked her why I was getting a new dress. "It's a surprise. You must wait and see." The moon was shining through our rice paper window. Holding onto Umma's arm, my mind was filled with dandelions, clovers, and a new dress. "I love you Soonyia." "I love you, Umma."

Chapter Four

Holt Adoption & Illness

"Good morning, my Princess," Umma whispered as she was waking me up. I like the way she tickled my neck. I wiggled and squealed and laughed until my sides hurt. We folded our comforters together and put them on the side of the room piled neatly. After I washed up by our well, my mom had a morning feast of rice, kimchee, and mackerel. Sometimes, the bone from the mackerel would lodge in my throat. My mom then made me take a huge bite of rice and gulp it down. It would then dislodge the bone from my throat. The dress my mom got for me had short puffy sleeves, ruffles, and shiny buttons on the front in a nice, long row. She then combed my hair and made it into a double ponytail. "Oh, I wish I had a camera to take a picture of you. You look so adorable." My mom and I boarded a bus in my new pretty dress. After a long ride, we arrived at our destination. There was a large black iron gate outside of this place with many flat roofed houses on a winding hill. I had not seen such flat roofed homes before, so this left a lasting impression on my young mind. Umma spoke with some adults there but I did not know what the grown-ups were saying but she hugged me and hugged me and told me that I had to stay – and then she was gone.

It was much later that I learned that Umma had taken me to live at the Holt International Adoption Agency. I loved playing with the other children there and having breakfast, lunch, supper, and even snacks each and every day! The house mothers at this place were very kind to me and the other children. My days were filled with playing with many children, but I missed my Umma the most when it was time for bed. I was away from my mom at an orphanage because she was unable to feed me. She used to say, "Soonyia, when you look at the moon, I will be looking at the same moon and thinking of you." The longer my Mom was away, my stomach no longer hurt from hunger, but I hurt in my heart for her. Umma, I miss you. When will you come for me? One day, while I was playing outside with my friends, I saw my mom motioning to me at the edge of the playground. I ran to her as fast as I could. She picked me up and quickly ran down the hill. She covered me with a scarf, told me not to say a word, and put me in a taxi. Everything happened very fast, but I felt very safe. I was again in my mother's arms and soon at our house. My Umma and I were together again.

As a special treat, my mom would give me a small bag of rice and some coins. With sheer delight we would walk towards the town market, hand in hand. After passing the bakery windows with red bean cakes, the butcher shop, and other stores and shops, we would begin to smell the smells and hear the sounds of our open-air market. Since we did not have a refrigerator, we needed to go to the market often to get our food. Squawking chickens crowded into crates while live fish were flapping their fins in the shallow water buckets. Fruits of all shapes and sizes were on display, as well as so many different vegetables. Farmers were selling fresh goods from baskets on their heads, bargaining with customers while some vendors shouted.

We finally came to a stall covered by an American parachute that sheltered many other foods and goods to sell. The aroma of popped rice gave me much anticipation as I handed my rice and the coins to the vendor. He would then put the raw rice into a ball shaped container with a little bit of salt. Next, he closed the lid and placed it over a hot fire turning and turning the container holding my rice. I would watch the whole time without taking my eyes away, waiting and listening for the 'pop-pop' to begin. When there was silence after many pops, the man would hand me the biggest bag of popped rice. How could such a small bag of raw rice make such a large bag of popped rice? How delightful this tasted! I rarely ate anything sugary, but when I tasted this popped rice, it was sweet to me. When I sucked on ants (pretty tasty, actually!!),

Typical Korean outdoor market sketched by Julie.

there was a sweet and sour appeal. Popped rice was nutty and sweet. Umma and I stood by the side of the tent, both reaching deep into the bag, munching and smiling at the same time. A small girl with hungry eyes came toward us. Before I had time to even think of sharing my treasure treat with her, she cupped her hands and looked at me as if to say, "May I have some, please?" It was good to see her smiling and enjoying some of the popped rice. I gave her more. I felt good to be able to share. I gave the girl more. But the poor girl would cough and cough. My mom shielded me from the coughing girl. She knew that many children had been getting sick recently. Walking back home carrying the leftover popped rice in a bag and holding my mom's hand talking and smiling, I felt we had everything we needed – more than we needed. We could share.

My mom loved to share, even when we did not have much – which was most of the time. Beggars would come to our house and she would share whatever we had. One time, my mom remarked what a nice scarf this beggar had. And then she saw that it moved! It was a snake around his neck! My mom did not like snakes. Nor did her daughter! As we left the market that day, we purchased a live chicken. When we got home, Umma had to try many times to grab the chicken till she was finally able to cut its head off. Even after the head was removed, the chicken ran around our pump! It was so funny trying to catch that headless chicken flapping around our small home. She was finally able to catch it and put it in the pot with the boiling water. Then she would take off the feathers and cook the chicken. We so enjoyed the feast!

Following our visit to the market, I started coughing and became sick. My mom went back and forth to the pump to get cold rags to put on my forehead. She was wiping my face and body to cool from fever. "How do you feel, Soonyia? Are you hungry?" "I don't know, Umma." I felt the comfort of my mom's cold rag but the coughing and coughing made my chest hurt. My Aunt Sughil came to visit. She was my mom's best friend. She always brought interesting news from the town. I could hear concern in my mom's voice as she was talking to Aunt Sughil. Aunt Sughil followed my mom's routine of cold rags and my mom went to the Buddhist temple to pray. Aunt Sughil's cigarette smoke quickly filled our small house, but when she realized I was coughing more, she put out the cigarette and threw it out the door. When my mom returned from the temple, she looked at Aunt Sughil and said," I've been praying every day, but Sooni is not getting better. I need to have a Shaman come and put the evil spirit out of our house."

The temple was on top of a mountain. When I went with my mom, we would have to climb a long, winding hill. The temple building was very colorful but the pictures of dragons and many gods with fierce eyes and swords in their hands scared me. Yet the monks were calm and friendly, often bowing to us. Umma told me not to be afraid. She said that the job of the dragons was to drive away the evil. We would bow to Buddha 108 times to get rid of "108 woes" in our lives. I remember we were not allowed to eat fish for a whole week before we went to the temple – nothing but rice and vegetables. This would please the gods, especially to celebrate Buddha's birthday on May 28. It was called 'the Feast of the Lanterns'.

To prepare for the Shaman coming, Umma folded our comforters neatly in the corner in front of the folded table and had the pretty side of the comforter showing. She cleaned the windowsill, floor, and the smudge on the door. She even tried to shine the pump and kitchen shelf. I asked Umma what Shaman did, she said, "When I lived with my parents in North Korea, the Shaman brought peace and healing to our village and talked to the spirits to make the sick person well."

When the Shaman came to our house, she wore a very colorful jacket of red, yellow, green, purple, and white with a long purple skirt decorated with many embroidered designs. She came with a man who was dressed in Korean ceremonial garb, having a tall black broad-brimmed round hat with his hair knotted inside. My mom gave whatever the money she had in her drawstring purse. Then this Shaman lit the incense in a bowl of raw rice. After she talked to my mom for a while, the man started playing a drum he had brought along – a drum which was large enough that he could beat it on either side. The Shaman began to dance, leaping up and down, jumping higher and higher, turning and chanting words that I did not understand. She swung her knife around the room, around the door, around the pump, around every square inch of our house. Meanwhile, the man kept playing the drum louder and louder. The Shaman asked me to jump. I had been too tired to even walk, yet somehow, I was jumping up and down next to her. After much dancing up and down, chanting and drum playing, they left. Our house was all quiet. What did all this mean? Would I get better now? And what made me jump so high? I was exhausted. Holding onto my mom's arm, I fell asleep.

I was lying on a damp comforter. It was hard to keep it dry with such a high fever and sweating. Outside our door, I could hear Umma speaking softly with Aunt Sughil, who had returned to inquire about my health. "Sooni's fever is not going away. Praying for her at the Buddhist temple and having the Shaman come to our home did not heal her. I only wish that I could have had the courage to leave Sooni at the Holt Orphanage. There was an American couple there who wanted to adopt Sooni – someone from Pennsylvania? I just couldn't let her go, even though I always wanted Sooni to go to America to get a good education. Now, she is so sick. What am I going to do? Sooni is my life!"

Some of what was said next was muffled, but I then heard Aunt Sughil say, "I am coming with you." My Auntie and my Mom took turns carrying me. They hurried to the health clinic to the left of Main Street, the same place where Umma went to get a note allowing her American GI friends to visit. I saw lots of strange-looking equipment. After the doctor listened to my Mom telling him the symptoms, he asked about the color of my urine. He was listening to my chest with a strange thing around his ears. Then he gave me a shot in my bottom. It was stinging! As we came out of the doctor's room, we saw many people lined up waiting. We must have been the first ones there this day. I could hear Umma and Auntie's quiet conversation. "Sooni needs lots of rest." I could hear Auntie whisper, "Tuberculosis. Children must be quarantined." I could see Umma's fear and I held onto her as tight as my weak body was able.

After Umma and Auntie Sughil took turns carrying me home from the clinic, Auntie asked my Mom whether she had certain herbs. When Auntie realized my mom did not have any, she went to the drug store next to our alley and bought some roots and herbs. I am usually curious about new things, but I was too tired and sick to care. The smell of the roots and herbs cooking made my stomach feel nauseated. Umma gave me that warm liquid to drink. It was so bitter, nothing like nutty sweet, popped rice. But I obeyed Umma and forced it down. I was sleepy and laid down and closed my eyes. But I could hear my mom and Auntie talking in low voices. "I am so afraid she might die," Umma cried.

"What about your dream for her?" Auntie asked. "In America, she'll have good medicine, a good home, and all the education she will want or need." "I tried," Umma answered. "I took her to Holt, but I could not leave her there. I just couldn't let her go. If I had not taken her away from Holt, she'd be in America already. She would not have the tuberculosis." For many weeks, my mom took me back to the health clinic. Some doctor always gave me shots in my bottom, which grew black and blue and hard from all the shots. I still coughed and felt tired, but I could feel that I was getting better - my comforter stayed drier. I was starting to get hungry and Umma's warm rice broth tasted smooth and nutty.

Chapter Five

School

In February of 1960, I was almost seven years old. "Soonyia," Umma pronounced my name with extended motherly pride and joy. "Let's get ready to go and register for school today!" Umma said the words that I wanted to hear ever since I felt better from the bout with tuberculosis. After getting ready, we walked through our alley and turned onto Main Street. After walking for some time, we came to the high gate of the elementary school. I looked at Umma. "This will be my school soon. Then I can study and learn many things." There were many other children with their parents to register for school. When it became our turn, the kind lady told us that I could not register because I did not have a family name.

In Korea at that time, only the father's family name is passed onto the children. "What is my father's family name?" My mom didn't know for sure. To her, he was 'Shorty.' Shorty Lieutenant. He was born across the ocean and was now back at his place of birth.

"Does that mean I am an American?"

"Koreans say that you are an American because your father is an American, but Americans say you are Korean because you were born in Korea."

"Who am I then? Korean or American? Will I be able to go to school?"

"Don't worry, Soonyia. We will pray that the gods will help us." On the way back home, Umma wanted to visit Father Goo. Many times, when Umma could not feed me, she took me to Father Goo's orphanage. He was always gentle and kind. I could eat with other children at his orphanage. After the Korean War, there were many orphans. My mom explained to Father Goo what happened at the school registration. He told us he would do his best to help us. My mom begged him, "Please, my daughter's entire future depends upon her getting an education." My mom was very concerned as we got home and tossed and turned all night.

We went back to see Father Goo the next day. He said, "Perhaps I can help you if you agree to take my family name." Bowing many times, my mom thanked Father Goo. "My daughter's name will be Goo Sooni!" The Koreans put the last name first because they consider the family name to be more important than the individual name. "I like my name, Umma!" After a successful registration, I was able to start first grade in March of 1960. My mom proudly purchased papers, pencils, scissors, and crayons. To celebrate, Umma said I could use some papers for practice and fun at home and save some for work at school.

I enjoyed drawing paper dolls. My mom would help me cut the dolls out. Then I drew a Hanbok, the Korean celebration dress which Umma also cut out for me. Then I folded the corners and dressed this paper doll with the Hanbok. I joyously danced around the room with my paper doll. Wearing a big smile, Umma could see how much I was looking forward to going to school. The next day, Umma and I went to our nearby mountain to gather pinecones. Each student was asked to bring at least two large bags of pinecones to use as kindling to fire up the wood stove in each classroom. My Mom and I were able to deliver what was asked of us before school started.

We had a special Korean Thanksgiving celebration at the end of September. It was called Ch'usok. Parents could come to school to join their children. My mom made this special rice cake filled with sesame seeds and other rice cakes filled with red beans, called songpyeon. My mom would lay pine needles before they were steamed. That special aroma filled our room with the pure and fresh fragrance of autumn. In the afternoon, there would be see-saw contests – seeing who could jump the highest on a see-saw. We also had wrestling competitions, chicken-fighting – who could knock their opponent down while both were standing on one foot. My favorite was the relay. I found out I could run pretty fast, and I usually came in second place. Having my mom at school, enjoying the special food and fun made my heart and tummy full!

During recess time at school, all the children were together on the playground playing kickball, jump rope, and tag. But I played alone. Some might have liked to play with me, but it was considered inappropriate to play with a person like me. I looked different from the rest of my classmates. My skin was lighter than theirs. My eyes were not almond shaped. My hair was much lighter than their jet-black hair. I was called "yellow-hair." Sometimes, when my mother could afford it, she would dye my hair black to make me look more like full-blooded Koreans.

At school, I felt I was free when I went on a swing. I would pump and pump to get as high as I could. I thought I was almost touching the clouds! Here, I was safe in my own little world. No one could touch me to taunt me for my looks while I was alone on a swing. The swing blew my light hair away from my face and my round-shaped eyes. My heart felt light.

As my swing was slowly coming to a stop, I saw a group of boys walking toward me. One of them was gripping the steel frame of the swing. They huddled and began to snicker and laugh as they pointed their fingers at me. They spoke loud enough that I could hear their mocking of my Umma for being friends with the GIs. Then one of the boys blurted out loudly, "That's why she's 'tigi." I wanted to cry out and say, "I'm not tigi! I am not less than a dog." But that dreaded word hurt again. No matter how many times I heard it before, it pierced my heart each time I heard it. I felt so angry. I wish I could yell back at them. I felt so choked up I couldn't even cry. My heart was pounding out of control. But I knew I must not fight back. The last time the kids teased and ridiculed me saying, "Yankee devil, go home!" my mom told me to walk away. "Buddha, please help me to walk away." One boy even said louder, "Tigi, dirty tigi!" Then the boy chanted together louder and louder, "Tigi! Tigi! Tigi!" Some even threw pebbles toward me. Some hit me, but most did not. The pebbles did not sting as much as their hurtful words. I closed my mouth tight. I was afraid if I would open it, I did not know what would come out. I must not look back. I must not cry. I must not let them know how much they hurt me. How can I comfort this heart of mine which only wants to burst?

I wish I could have told my teacher about what happened on the playground. But she did not look like me. Perhaps she would not understand. My teacher was nice. But was she nice to my face only? Does she think I am a tigi like my classmates say? My teacher did not put me down. She treated everyone the same. Learning came easy for me and I did well in school. At least I could not be teased for not working hard or doing well in school. I liked the smile on Umma's face when I came home with good grades. For a treat, she would often give me piggy-back rides and spin me around which I loved. We sometimes got spanked in class. If one person did something wrong, the entire class was disciplined. Consequently, everyone tried to be good. No one wanted to be responsible for the entire class being spanked with a ruler. A million times I wanted to tell my teacher about the ridicule I received from my classmates. But I could not bear the possible rejection by my teacher and the other kids being upset at me for getting them punished. So, I did not say anything.

Being at school among all pure Koreans made me feel like a half-breed for the first time. I began to believe that something was missing. Something was desperately wrong with me. My loneliness caused the school day to never seem to end. I enjoyed the learning and the work, but the lack of relationships with my classmates made the walk home such a welcomed relief at the end of the day. I walked as fast as I could carrying my books and thinking of all that happened on the playground. I ran through the alleyway to open our rice paper door. As soon as I saw my mom, a flood of tears soaked my face. She hugged me and hugged me some more. She wiped my tears and put me on her lap. I saw the sad look on her face and I knew she understood. At that moment, I felt as though it was my mom and me against the world. I was all she had, and she was all I had. In each other, we felt comfort and love beyond words. As my hurting heart lessened, I would tell her word for word what had happened that day.

Umma hugged me close. "I love you, Soonyia. Oh, how I love you! You are so special to me. Do not believe it when others tease you. Just ignore them." She snuggled me on her lap and I asked her why I was made like this with lighter hair, lighter skin, and round eyes. "Why can't I have black hair, darker skin, and almond-shaped eyes like the other children?" Umma hugged me again and told me it was because my father was not Korean. He was an American soldier who came to save us from our enemies. "Please tell me more. Tell me the whole story of my father."

Umma's eyes began to tear. She tried to hold it in, but the more she tried, the more she cried. I hugged her and said, "Don't cry. I love you so much. We don't have to talk about my father now." When I was younger, we had a picture of my father. But Umma said that one day a candle tipped over toward the rice paper window. The wall paper quickly started on fire. His picture was one of the items that burned that night. Any glimpse of what he might have looked like disappeared. Did I look like him? Does he have a picture of me? Does he ever think about me?

Would I have teased mixed-race children if I were full Korean? Until the 1950's Amerasians were unknown to Koreans. Does the unknown create fear and fear create prejudice? If I were full Korean, would I have said that Amerasians were inferior? "They are not as good as me." Through hundreds of years of history, the Korean people had never witnessed these fatherless, nameless, and shoeless Amerasian children. They looked at us as shame that their daughters had committed. Today, after all these years that I have been in America, how do I feel towards the Korean people? They are my people. They are my mother's people. I have no ill feelings, but only that of understanding. Other school children saw me as different. Being different can lead to prejudice. Prejudice can lead to fear. Fear can lead to hatred. Children did not know better. I suppose their parents did not know better either.

Chapter Six

MP, Monsoon & Mountain

Our classroom was filled with the aroma of kimchee and rice in the lunch boxes of students. We kept them on top of the pot belly stove to keep warm. But I knew none of those lunches belonged to me. I didn't have any lunch to bring to school that day. The smell, especially of the kimchee, made my stomach long for food, any food!

My kind teacher gave a few of us students without lunches a piece of round bread. I was so thankful she had bread for us when we had nothing. I wanted to study hard to become a kind teacher like my teacher or the nice doctor who helped me when I had tuberculosis. I wanted to help others. That afternoon, I saw my teacher going to the restroom. I remember being so surprised. Teachers were like gods to me. To my young mind, teachers were above the need to use the lavatory facility.

One Friday, I was hoping that a G.I. friend would come so that Umma could buy some food for us. While I was playing stone jacks in the alley, a military police (MP) came to Umma's door. He wanted to see my mom's medical papers. She had not felt well lately and she wasn't able to get her medical papers stamped at the clinic.

The MP escorted my mom out of the house as I cried, "Ummaaaa!" He passed me by the alley as I followed Umma. He took Umma to the truck with the open back. On one side was a bench where the other aunties were sitting. I ran toward the truck, just to touch Umma's hand and the truck began to move. Umma was calling, "Soonyia!" and I screamed her name just as before.

She was gone. Only the dust from the truck remained. Running as fast as I could, I no longer was able to keep up with the truck. As I turned left toward our alley, two boys walking by yelled, "Round eyes! Tigi!

Tigi!" I pretended not to hear and walked as fast as I could to our alley and our one room house – alone.

It was unusually quiet at Mamasan's house that evening. I was so very hungry, and I was scared. Some of the cold rice from the morning was still in the pot. I used my fingers to scrape rice from the sides while licking my fingers. I washed the pot and put it next to the shelf. With my scooped hands, I drank as much water as I could.

I pulled out the comforters and lay down and stared at the moon beaming through the window. My mom always said, "When you look at the moon, I will be looking at the same moon and thinking of you."

I love you, Umma. I miss you. Will the MP bring Umma back? I do not want to think of living without Umma. I prayed to the gods that she would come home tomorrow.

The farmer's rooster crowed his daily, "Gho-gkee-oh," to announce the start of a new day. Rubbing my eyes, I listened for the sound of my mom. Perhaps she is cooking in the kitchen, splashing water at the pump, or talking to the Aunties. But I did not hear a sound. All was quiet, except for the sound of my crying. I was so afraid as I folded the comforter and put it next to the table where I placed it every morning.

I emptied the potty into the ditch where the leftover pumped water goes. This is my least favorite chore. Next, I sprinkled salt on my finger and rubbed my teeth clean followed by splashing water on my face to wake up my sleepy eyes. I pumped more water into my cupped hands and drank until I could drink no more.

I gathered my books and homework from yesterday and went to school. Saturdays were half-days at school. But I could not concentrate on school lessons. My mind was consumed with my mom and my hunger pangs. It was the longest half-day ever.

I walked as fast as I could on Main Street and ran through the alley, opened the rice paper covered door as fast as I could. There was my mom sitting legs crossed and waiting for me to sit on her lap. We burst into tears, hugging each other so tight. Umma had come home. My love. My life.

In Korea, the monsoon season is from June to August. As the rising of the sun comes each day, the monsoon batters us each year. Some years, it rains constantly for about forty days. This "Jangma" can be a friend or a foe. Sometimes, the rain comes down so fast that our road can be flooded almost immediately. The long duration of humidity would create mildew on our bedroom wall. My Mom would try to clean it, but it kept coming back. Last night's storm subsided but I could see rain clouds in the distance.

School did not cancel because of the rain. In class we discussed the cause and effect of the monsoon. I wondered what would happen to our town if the monsoon destroyed the rice again? One year, we had such a bad monsoon that mud poured down from the mountain and destroyed much of the farmers' rice crops. Food was scarce. Government help was slow to come. Only people with a lot of money could buy rice. Poor people like my mom had no means to purchase rice. No free vegetables could be found.

In desperation, Umma and I stripped bark off a tree to pull the inner fibers of the tree. We would bring it home, cut it, put in the pot and boil it with water. This would be our dinner. It would give us the momentary satisfaction of being full, but sometimes it would give us a stomach ache. I often wonder why I ate it again and again? I wished that we had Aunties' scraps but they didn't have food or customers either. I guess the moment of true hunger was too much to bear. Anything remotely edible would do.

The rain again began with a few drops followed quickly by the fierce, pounding rain. My teacher told us she suspected that it will be a huge storm today. "Please pack your things. Go directly home. Be safe, everyone!" I was supposed to go to Halmauni's house today after school. I know she would let me stay with her overnight, if need be. I packed my things carefully, said good-bye to my teacher, and ran toward the gate. What a relief to see Umma by the school gate. "Water is filling the creeks and ditches in Pubwon-ni," Umma said. I cannot let you go to Halmauni's alone. We will both go to her and be safe."

Umma and I hurried toward the path along a creek toward Halmauni's farm. Our wet clothes clung to our sopping wet bodies. The water from the muddy creek reached beyond its banks in such a short time and rose to our ankles. We squished each time we took steps in our rubber shoes, sweating from the heat and humidity, carrying my books in a bag on top of my head while holding onto it with one hand. Umma and I rolled up our pants. It was hard to walk fast through the rising water. Umma and I knew every stepping stone normally used to cross the creek. I played and bathed by this creek. The water continued to rise. We rolled up our pants as high as they would roll. It was hard to see the stepping stones through the muddy, rising water. "Umma, how can we cross this? I'm scared." Umma then proceeded to carry me on her back as she used to piggy back me when I was a child. I had one hand on my book bag and another around Umma's neck. I hugged her as tightly as I could as she stepped into the stream. "Don't be afraid, Soonyia. I have you. "Ummmaaaahhhh!" I screamed.

Suddenly, the overflow pushed us further downstream. "Somebody, help us!" my mom screamed. "Soonyia, don't let my hand go! God, please help us!" We tried to push the water away to reach a tree trunk ahead that had fallen into the rushing water. At the same time, I was holding onto Umma's one hand for dear life. My book bag had drifted away already. The tree root was still lodged in the soil, so I knew if I could reach it, we would have a life line. "Umma, a tree! Let's grab it. God is helping us." Umma grabbed at the tree trunk and pulled me toward the shore. Umma was able to gain a foothold and we were able to regain our breath. We then could climb out of the fierce flowing stream and up onto the bank. Soaking wet and weary, we followed the muddy road to Hamauni's house. We said thank you to the god who saved us!

Finally, the monsoon season was over and it was Fall. Umma put me to bed one night with these words, "Soonyia, it's time for the chestnuts to be falling. How I love to eat chestnuts! We will leave early tomorrow morning for the mountain, right after breakfast. Get some sleep, Soonyia!" Holding onto my Umma's arm, being cozy in our comforters, I could feel her warmth. She would often rub my back, soothing a hard day away. "Umma, you rub my back so good!" "I learned how to give massages when I worked for a Japanese family, when they controlled our Korean people. The Japanese acted very harshly toward our people for many years. Sometimes people like to put other people down to elevate themselves," Umma said.

"Is that like people calling me tigi? And, yankee devil go home?" "Yes, Soonyia, just ignore them. They are not used to the American lighter skin and round eyes." "Like my father's eyes?" "Yes, Soonyia. Your eyes are beautiful and I love you so much." "I love you too, Umma." So much to think about, but for now, my mom's loving arms around me and I dreamed of chestnuts! All is well.

While we were on our way to the mountain, I saw a girl about my age riding a bicycle. "Umma, can I have a bike someday?" With unusual firmness, Umma blurted, "No!" "Why not?" "You'll ruin yourself." "How? Why can't I ride a bike?" "The bike might change your insides. Someday, when you marry, I want your husband to know you are a virgin." Even though I was only eleven years old, I understood how important it was to my mom that I stay a virgin until I got married. She spoke often of it. She also kept telling me how important it was to get an education, be adopted, and live in America – the land of opportunity. Umma would say that out of this ditch, she and many of my aunties could never escape.

My mind filled with thoughts of what Umma said and I didn't realize that we were almost to our favorite mountain. In the heat of the summer, this mountain is where my mom and I would often lie under the shade of a tree watching the leaves dance through the sun rays and listening to the crickets chirping. Today, they were giving a concert! As the weather got hotter, they chirped even louder and more rapidly. As hard as I tried to count their chirps, I could not keep up. "Umma, look at the chestnut tree over there." Under this beautiful tree, some of the spiny hulls, looking like porcupine quills fell. In my mom's scarf we gathered the chestnuts which fell onto the ground.

Umma said, "Gather the ones that have spiny burs split open. "Why not the others, I asked?" Umma said, "When they are green and closed, the nuts inside are not ripe." "Is that why you don't want me to climb the tree and shake the branches?" "Yes. We need to be patient and wait for them to be ripe and fall."

It was fun to press down with my feet while poking with a stick just enough to release the chestnuts. But the burrs are very sharp and we had to be extremely careful not to prick our hands. If I did, blood would start to drip from my fingers. But, when we got three nuts per burr, it was worth it! The morning gathering of the chestnuts was profitable. But I was anxious to go home and boil the chestnuts so we could eat them. This morning's thin rice soup and yesterday's leftover dandelions didn't stay in my belly too long.

We climbed a little higher in the mountain to our water spring. We cupped our hands, filled them with the cool water, and drank heartily. I splashed my face with the cold water and I drank some more and more until my hunger went away. How this water flowing between the rocks could quench my thirst and hunger with its sweetness!

When we arrived home, my mom would use her knife to make slits in each chestnut. Then they would be placed in the water to be boiled. Once they were boiled, she would drain all the water and leave the lid open. When cooled, we both sat cross-legged under our low table and feast on warm chestnuts. It took a long time to eat each chestnut since we had to peel a couple of layers before we could eat them. Though it kept us from devouring the chestnuts too quickly, we were hardly patient with the peeling. My mom said with a big smile, "Soonyia, let's go again to the mountain tomorrow. I saw more burrs on the branches ready to drop. We should go earlier tomorrow before the squirrels and other hungry animals get to the chestnuts!"

Chapter Seven

Happy Orphanage

Aunt Sughil come to visit us. I loved hearing her interesting ideas and news of our town. I am glad my mom has a good girl friend with whom she can confide and share. "How have you been feeling, Songja?" Aunt Sughil asked my mom as Umma was puffing on her cigarette. "Not too well," my mom replied. "My bleeding just doesn't seem to stop. I haven't been able to work. The money we saved is dwindling and I am concerned for Sooni." "I heard that in Munsanyup, near Camp Rose, an orphanage just opened," Auntie said. "I heard that the American G.I.'s are funding the place. There are many good-hearted G.I.'s."

"My father was a G.I., too," I chimed in. "Yes, he was," mom said. "A very kind-hearted man. That is why you are so sweet, Soonyia." "Someday, when I go to America, I might get to see him. Would he recognize me, Umma?" "We have to wait and see," Umma said. Auntie told us that we should both go to check out the orphanage.

My mom tossed and turned. She was not feeling too well. I held onto my mom's arm while she rubbed my back with her other arm. We comforted each other. "Umma, I love you! I hope you feel better soon."

Like clockwork, the rooster crowed, "Gho-gkee-oh." I rubbed my eyes open while lying still, but Umma was still so tired even after a night of sleep. She said, "Soonyia, should we go and visit Happy Orphanage today?" "If you think it's best, let's do that, Umma," I replied.

Umma was moving much slower this morning. After eating some rice and kimchee, we tidied up and put on the same clothes we had on the past few days – the best we had. We rubbed some water to lessen the wrinkled look. Our hair was combed carefully. We took some money from Umma's drawstring purse and left our house through the dark alley.

Even in the morning, this alley always seemed to be dark from the tall drug store wall which blocked the sun. Soon the bright sun met us and led us to the bus station at Mickey Mouse corner.

The bus station always seemed to have buses parked waiting to depart. It was a busy place with people from neighboring towns arriving and many from Pubwon-ni departing. Since I was eleven years old, I've been able to shine shoes and sell gum at this bus station to help my mom buy more rice. I knew that all the kids who shined shoes were boys. We called them the 'shoeshine boys.' Even the G.I. compound had shoeshine boys to keep their boots clean. I was the first 'shoeshine girl' I knew. I was able to keep up. Moving my arms back and forth so fast, I could make the shoes shine even more. I only shined shoes on Saturdays after school and on Sundays. Some customers were amazed to see a shoe shine girl. The G.I.'s were kind toward me and gave me more money than I asked. When they saw my light hair and round eye, they knew I was one of them. G.I. friends called my mom "Mickey" because she lived by the Mickey Mouse Corner. They knew she was the mother of an Amerasian girl. As I worked hard to shine the G.I.'s boots, I thought, "Would my Dad look like him? Where are you, Shorty? We need you and miss you so much!"

While shining shoes, I also had a small wooden box next to me filled with chewing gum. Sometimes, G.I. friends brought me gum, too. With money I earned, I could purchase more gum from the drug store. My customers would often buy a piece or two of gum after their shoes were polished. Some became my regular customers. I wonder whether they liked my service or felt sorry for a young Amerasian girl trying to buy rice. One time, though, a Korean man put his shoe on top of the box and when his eyes met mine, he said, "Oh…you are one of those. I will go to another shoeshine boy." All I could do was to stop the burst of tears. I told myself I must hold it in. I must not let others see my tears. Another customer came, and I polished his shoes. I have no memory of it. I was so upset. It was all a blur.

I came home and I looked into our small mirror. Trying to withhold my tears, I observed my features. "Oh, why am I made this way? What is wrong with me? Why aren't there many kids looking like me? The darker, curly haired girl who beats me in the races is the only one who looks like me." Umma came in the room and sensed something was wrong with me. She gave me a big hug and in her loving arms, I burst into tears. I told Umma what had happened. "Umma, can you change my face and my hair color?" My mom gazed at me and said, "The gods made you just right. You are special, and I love you with all of my heart. You are my princess."

Our bus to Munsanyup was ready to depart. My Mom and I sat next to each other holding hands pondering what today would bring. Our bus kicked up much dust on the dirt on the stone-filled road. As we traveled, our bus moved from side to side and up and down on the bumpy road. The ride to Happy Orphanage did not seem too far.

We came to a two-story building made of grey blocks. I could see a dirt-covered open field. We walked through a middle door to where the orphanage father's office was. He was wearing a western suit with a tie. His black hair was combed back. He greeted us with a warm smile and showed us the place. The downstairs had a few rooms where children lived and the upstairs was the place where students did their school work. Off to the side of that large building was where they ate. Nearby, the orphanage father and his wife had a separate house.

I did not want to be separated from my mom, but she felt that since I was getting older and she was not able to provide sufficient food for me, it would be good for me to stay at Happy Orphanage and go to school there. I was allowed to go see my mom on some weekends. That news made my achy heart feel better. I started my sixth-grade year at Happy Orphanage in March of 1965.

There were about 30-40 children in our dormitory with three or four house moms who cooked and cared for us. My new found friend, Jun Soon, had her mother there working for us as a cook. When my mom inquired if she could also work there and be near me, she found out there were no more positions. How wonderful it would have been if Umma had been allowed to work there.

For many weeks, all the children at the orphanage have been practicing singing, 'Holy, Holy, Holy, Lord God Almighty.' But I had no idea, absolutely no idea what we were singing. Not knowing any English, I was just mouthing the sound. I liked when Jun Soon sat behind me. She was a good singer and I could try to mimic what she was saying.

Our whole orphanage group were often invited to either Camp Rose or Camp Knox. We went to some other G.I. compounds, too, but I do not remember the names. We would sit in front of the G.I. compound and all sing 'Holy, Holy, Holy.' I could see G.I.'s smiling but wondered if they could understand what we were singing. I certainly did not!

A G.I. in a robe talked and talked in English. I had no idea what he was talking about, but I saw the soldiers listening to what he was saying. What I did understand and enjoy was going to the cafeteria after the chapel service. We would line up and get a tray with a plate to fill with whatever food they provided for us. We would eat until our tummies were full. This was a feeling I was not accustomed to. I was very thankful. My father must have worked in places like this. Umma told me that he was Shorty Lieutenant who took care of the cafeteria in Pusan.

I was sitting next to Jun Soon, my new friend. She was a few years older than me, but very kind. "Jun Soon, what does G-O-D mean?" "It means Ha Nan Nim, God of the Bible," Jun Soon explained to me. It is the God that Christians believe in. They believe God created the heavens and the earth and us, too." "Do you believe that, Jun Soon?" I asked. "Yes," she simply replied. I said, "My Mom prays to the gods of Buddha. Sometimes the pictures of the gods of the temple scare me."

It was at either Camp Rose or Camp Knox that a chaplain was very kind to me. Perhaps he was an assistant chaplain at one of these compounds. He was a 'big brother' to me, talking to me, smiling with me, and giving me goodies to take back to the orphanage with me. Singing 'Holy, Holy, Holy' and seeing this chaplain became the two biggest reasons I looked forward to chapel each Sunday.

One day, my chaplain friend came to Happy Orphanage driving a jeep. With the consent of the orphanage father, the chaplain took me to the snack bar at his army compound. He bought me hamburgers and French fries. I remember thinking it was the tastiest food I had ever had.

Then he took me to a movie theater on base. On the screen there was a guy playing the guitar and singing. There was also a pretty red-haired lady who sang and danced. I thought she was the most beautiful woman I had ever seen. During the movie I turned around to see a large wheel turning with a light attached to allow us to see the movie. I learned later that the movie was called "*Viva Las Vegas*" starring

Julie, Big Brother GI and Jun Soon.

Elvis Presley and Ann-Margret. I had never seen a man move his hips like that!

Then, this big brother wanted me to show him where my mother lived. We drove in his jeep to Mickey Mouse Corner and walked the alley to my small home. This big brother introduced himself to my mom and handed her a lot of money to help take care of us. After he returned me to the Happy Orphanage, he gave me a huge hug. "God bless you," he said. I never saw him again. Oh, how good he was to my mom and me. How I wish I could find him and thank him for all he meant to me and for his goodness and kindness. I do have a picture of the kind chaplain, Jun Soon, and me in the chapel. But I never knew his name. I shared his picture with many soldiers who were in Korea, hoping they might remember him. "Someday, God, I would love to find this kind G.I. chaplain and thank him for how good he was to me and to my mom before leaving for his home in America."

One of the chores that Jun Soon and I needed to perform at Happy Orphanage was to scoop dung from the outhouse and spread it over the vegetable gardens to fertilize the soil. Jun Soon and I used a big scooper and put dung into two small buckets. When they were about two-thirds full, we would put a long rod through the handles of those two buckets, and put the center of the rod over our shoulders to carry to the vegetable garden. Or, we would put the two buckets in the middle of the rod and carry them by holding the edge of the rod together. We didn't like to be too close to the buckets. They had a putrid smell. Even when we washed again and again by the creek running next to the edge of our garden, the smell never seemed to go away. But the house moms told us that we were making the vegetables happy so they grew faster. The outhouse we had was very much like the public outhouse we had by our house near

Mickey Mouse Corner. At our house, when I came out the door, I would turn left to follow the ditch where our overflow from the water pump would go. I always hoped people would leave dry pieces of paper near the ditch that I could use to wipe. Sometimes I would use leaves. But, at our Happy Orphanage, we had softer papers to use. I wondered if the American soldiers gave them to us. Inside the outhouse, there was a wooden plank which had a big hole. It was on top of a big round container. I heard that the G.I.'s gave that to us as well. Once in a while, our teacher would give us a big white pill to take to de-worm. We were asked to report how many worms came out of us when we went to the outhouse. I often counted three or four. Some of the boys in the classroom seemed to compete. They would boast of five or six worms when they went to the outhouse.

At Happy Orphanage, we would put our comforters in a row in the bedroom to sleep. About a dozen children would be in each room with a house mom. When one got lice, we would all get lice! When my hair was infested with lice, Jun Soon's mom sprinkled a lot of DDT (Dichlorobiphenyl Trichloroethane) insecticide on my hair. Then she mixed it all around my hair and wrapped my head in a towel. While the lice were dying, my head itched so badly! I thought I was going mad. I was not allowed to take the towel off so I started pounding my head to stop itching. The DDT killed all the lice, but not the eggs that were laid by the adult female lice. It was so hard to get rid of them because they were stuck to the hair shaft so tightly. Jun Soon's mom used a very tight comb to comb them out, but that was difficult and painful. So, Jun Soon's mom told me that it would be better for me if she shaved all of my hair down to the scalp. I looked like a monk at the Buddhist temple! The monks always looked somber and serene in their robes and shaved heads, but the bloody scalp from lice eating into my skin did not look so good. As a sixth-grade girl, I was devastated!

We had three meals a day at Happy Orphanage. That was much more than I was used to. Our menu consisted of lots of bean sprout soup, turnip soup, and kimchee soup. I was so thankful.

One day, my nose took me to a wonderful smell that was coming out of the orphanage father's house. His lovely wife was making scallion pancakes with sesame oil. I remember wishing so much I could eat some

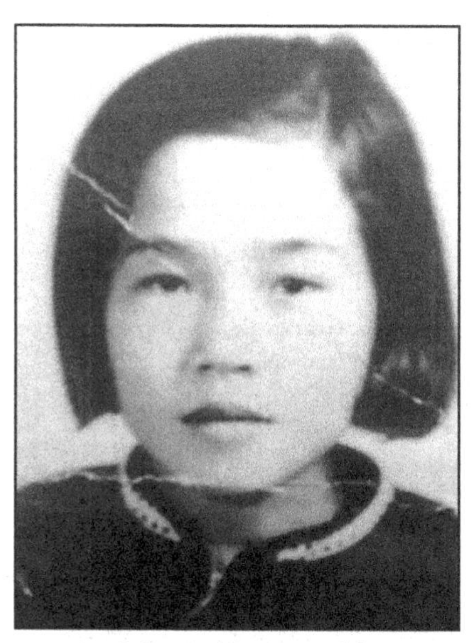

Julie at 11 years old.

of that. His wife was so beautiful and her skin so silky. Jun Soon told me that she washes her skin with the milk we get from the American soldiers. As much as I liked the pretty wife of the orphanage father, I did not think it was right if she was using milk meant for us to be washing her skin.

At our recess time, we often played kickball. I loved to run, kick, and move. Once, as I was running as fast as I could to a base, I ran over a stone and tripped. I fell to the ground in pain with a sprained ankle. It was bad enough that I was taken to the dispensary at Camp Rose. The doctor tried to take good care of me, but the sprain was not quickly healing. When I went to see my mom with my crutches, she said, "Soonyia, I am going to take you to an acupuncturist tomorrow. It's been too long that your ankle hasn't been well." The acupuncturist had a long beard and hair knotted inside of a hat. He was wearing a tall round-brimmed black hat like the man who came with Shaman. He was in white, ceremonial Korean garb. He took out many needles and asked me about all the places where my ankle hurt. He then placed these long needles into my skin. At one time, there were up to a dozen needles in my lower leg and ankle. The needles were so long and they seemed to sway. How could all these needles help? He must have been understood my doubts because he calmly said, "I am trying to eliminate your painful sensations." Strangely enough, I was able to walk out of his house not needing the crutch. Umma said with a big smile, "I will carry the crutch for you." We both thanked the doctor by bowing our heads many times. To this day, I wonder how he did that!

Once, we were asked to put on a play at one of the G.I. compounds. I do not remember the name or what the play was about, but I think I was one of the main characters. I was a bird who had a broken leg and danced as a "hurting bird."

At Happy Orphanage, I enjoyed competing using my abacus while the G.I. used his adding machine. I had been using an abacus for many years. I often defeated the adding machine with my abacus. Those competitions were so much fun!

Happy Orphanage
Julie at bottom right with arms around two younger classmates.

Chapter Eight

New School & The D's House

My sixth-grade year at the Happy Orphanage was completed sometime in February, 1966. I was able to go home to my Umma. I missed her warm smiles, loving hugs, and lying together in our shared comforters holding onto her one arm while she rubbed my back as I fell asleep. Umma always gave me all she had to take care of me. I was her life. She was mine. I missed the moonbeam shining through the window as we thought of my father.

It was good to see Mamasan's rosy, pleasingly plump cheeks. The Aunties welcomed me back and were glad to have "our rose in the ditch" home again. It was so good to see Aunt Sughil and Halmauni and her pigs. I was so thankful that my mom was feeling much better. The doctors from the health clinic helped my mom to get well. I was so thankful of the goodness of so many people around me. Everywhere I went, my face told of my past, my beginning. Some may tease, ridicule, spit, and call me all kinds of names suggesting that I have no worth and am not wanted. But I chose to think of the goodness in people. I also wanted to work hard in school so I could help others someday. Around Umma, the Aunties, and our small circle of friends, I felt at home and accepted.

Since I came home from Happy Orphanage, I was not able to go to any school. "Soonyia, I don't know what we are going to do. You are of age to go to junior high school, but we don't have any money to send you. My dream always has been for you to go to America and get a good education. I am so sorry, Soonyia!" It was time for me to enter 7th grade, but we had no means for me to go to school. The Korean government at that time only provided free education through grade school. From seventh grade up, it was just like going to college in America. A prospective junior high school student first must pass a particular exam to meet Korea's rigorous academic standards. Then the family had to pay tuition, purchase books, and buy special uniforms for school. There was no way I could ever continue my education.

Julie's sketch of Umma and Julie washing clothes at the creek.

Since I was not going to go to school, I had more time to shine shoes, sell gum, and wash others' clothes by the creek to help my mom buy rice. We carried the baskets filled with dirty clothes on top of our heads. My mom could balance the basket so well, she did not even need to place her hand on one side of the basket. I, on the other hand, needed much assistance. When we arrived at the creek, we needed to find a spot away from where other ladies were cleaning. We then would rub the dirty spots against the stones. We would carry the washed clothes in our baskets and hang them on the line to dry. There was just enough room to hang the line in our tiny space near our home.

I enjoyed helping Umma by earning some money, but my mom was truly concerned with what was going to happen to me. I could sense her concern and sadness. No Korean man in his right mind would marry a mixed-race person like me with my looks and no proper family. Without an education, my future looked bleak. My mom truly did not want me to be a part of the world she was unable to escape. She didn't want me to live in a ditch and follow her steps. "Oh, God. Please help us!" we would pray.

One day we had a visitor at our door. This young lady was in western clothes and introduced herself as Miss Moon. She was very petite with short black hair. She said she was a social worker representing the Pearl S. Buck Foundation in Sosa. When she arrived at our town looking for mixed-race children, she told us she had no problem finding where we lived. People said, "You mean Sooni? I'll tell you where she lives."

Miss Moon told us that Pearl Buck was a Nobel Prize-winning author who had grown up in China, the daughter of American Christian missionaries. Evidently, she was also discriminated against in China while growing up with blue eyes and blonde hair. Pearl S. Buck had started a foundation in Korea to provide education for Amerasian children. The goal, Miss Moon told us, was to allow the Amerasian children to grow to be more productive citizens in their mother countries. Amerasian children, we were told, were sponsored by many generous and kind-hearted Americans.

Miss Moon asked Umma, "Would you like Sooni to be educated in Sosa at the Pearl S. Buck Foundation Opportunity School?" Umma quickly answered, "Oh yes! Please. I've been so praying to the gods that Sooni would be able to go to school." A concerned look crossed Miss Moon's friendly face when she heard that I was ready to start junior high school because the Pearl S. Buck Foundation only has an elementary school nearby – not the junior high school that I needed. As she left, Miss Moon said she would do whatever she could to help me find a place for school. Umma and I were really worried.

However, Miss Moon returned in a few days letting us know that a plan was in place for me to continue schooling. She told us that I would be living with an American couple that lived in Seoul. I will be going to a school near their house, but I must first pass the junior high school's exam to meet their academic standards. My mom assured Miss Moon, "Sooni will do well. She loves learning and loves school." We were so thankful for this new opportunity that was presented before me. My mom packed all my things in a small bag and prepared to send me away to an

American home to live in while I attended school in Seoul. I had a comb, hair pin, undergarments, pencils, and the clothes on my back.

In January 1967, Miss Moon, my mom, and I got on the bus and went to my new home in Seoul, belonging to the kind 'Mr. and Mrs. D.' Once we got off the bus, we had to go through the gate to walk to their house. It was a 'gated' community where many Americans who worked in Seoul resided. I was so anxious to meet Mr. and Mrs. D. What would they be like? I could also see the anxiousness in Umma's face.

Mrs. D. was tall and had short, dark hair. Mr. D had a round face but no hair. I liked his warm smile. They welcomed us and showed us where my room would be. My new room was lovely with curtains and it was bigger than our one room house in Pubwon-ni! Their home was wonderful, but I wished so in my heart that my mom would not have to go back to her home many miles away. Though I knew how much Umma wanted me to get an education, tears filled my eyes as I watched my mom and Miss Moon leave on the bus.

Mr. and Mrs. D could not speak Korean and I spoke no English. Although I understood some words, we did a lot of smiling and pointing. When they realized that I did not have any clothes to change into, Mr. and Mrs. D took me to an army PX and their gated community's market. I saw many, many things that I had never seen before. I felt like I was Cinderella trying on many pretty clothes. We purchased some more undergarments, and then Mrs. D. said that I needed a bra. I was measured by a store assistant and was fitted for a bra for the very first time. It was so kind of Mrs. D to purchase clothes for me. But the dresses that I liked, she did not purchase. She said, "My sewing woman can make dresses for you." I was disappointed to see those dresses go back on the rack!

After a few days, Miss Moon came to take me to an all girls' school in Seoul. She said, "Sooni, you need to do your very best on this exam. You can only go to this school if you pass the test." I assured her I would try my very best. In the classroom, there were all girls seated by their desks. I could feel the tension in the room. I know I needed to do my best and make my mom proud of me. Miss Moon came again to pick me up after the exam. I liked her a lot. She was kind and took great interest in me. After taking a bus and then walking for ten to fifteen minutes, we came to the main building of the school. There were already many people waiting for the result of the exam that had been taken. We kept looking for Goo Sooni's results. My heart was beating fast. And, then there was my name! I passed the exam and was accepted into this all-girls Han Yang Dae Huk Go Junior High School. We then went to the school store, purchased a blue uniform with a white collar, white sneakers, and a book bag. Miss Moon paid for it all. She told me that these purchases were being taken care of by my American sponsor in America. I thought, "How good a person to educate someone else when they have not yet even met that person." My heart was filled with gratefulness toward my mom, Miss Moon, Mr. and Mrs. D, and the sponsor in America whom I did not know.

Soon after I started school, Mrs. D informed me that my bedroom was changing. She told me that Mrs. Choon, her seamstress, needed a bigger space to work. She was given my bedroom to work and to sleep. Already, my bedroom was filled with Mrs. Choon's personal things. My new room was now on the porch. "When the cook needs to sleep overnight, she will use the top bunk and you will sleep in the bottom." I'm sure Mrs. D needed a bigger room for the seamstress but it saddened my heart to lose the big room that I had for only a few days. I reminded myself how fortunate I was to have all the opportunities that I had living at Mr. and Mr. D's and now I was going to a junior high school.

Mrs. Choon measured me and measured twice. And she made me two beautiful dresses. One dress was blue and yellow with a sailor's collar and the other was a blue dress with a white collar and a bright, colorful tie. I said, "Mrs. D, thank you so very much! Mrs. Choon, thank you so very much! I can't wait until my Umma can see these dresses." Then Mrs. D said, "Mr. D and I would like to take you to see your mom tomorrow." I was so glad to hear her say that and I thanked her in English. That's something I learned because of how nice Americans had been to me. It was fun to ride in a car instead of a bus. Except for the time my mother had taken me from the Holt orphanage in a taxi, this was the only car ride I had ever taken. I soon found out that even riding in Mr. D's car, we went from side to side and bumped up and down as we hit the uneven spots.

My mom was beyond glad to see all of us. Some of the townspeople gathered by the road side to see the car and American couple that had brought me there. Due to her overwhelming gratitude, Umma gave Mrs. D the best thing she had – the rice container my father had given her before he went back to America. My mom kept bowing and bowing to Mr. and Mrs. D. Mr. D had brought his camera and he took some pictures of my mom and me. I was so grateful that for the first time, we had a picture of us.

Julie and Umma
Jung Song Ja

I was able to visit my mom almost every other weekend and I became very good at knowing what bus to take. I longed to see her! The bus ride was long, but it felt like an eternity until I could be with her. On one of my bi-weekly visits, my mom seemed unusually saddened about something. She kept hugging and kissing me. She even said, "Don't go, Soonyia. I miss you so." She cried when I left her to go back to Mr. and Mrs. D's. She desperately wanted me to stay with her longer.

My new junior high school started sometime in March of 1967. I wore my uniform, had my hair in a barrette, and my new white sneakers on my feet. Before I entered the school gate, the upper-class students checked to see that I had no make-up, no nail polish, and no jewelry. They checked to see that our sneakers were white and clean, our hair was just the right length, and only one barrette. I liked wearing uniforms. They made us all look the same…almost! We could show our individuality by what we do and what we say, and by our character rather than what we wore.

School work was both challenging and stimulating. I was so thankful that my former teachers prepared me so well. In my English classroom, some students said, "You are good in English because you look like 'American.'" Does one speak a language because he looks like he should be from that country? English was a required course in seventh grade. Students worked diligently to learn English, as they did in all their subjects. Often, they went to a second school after school to enrich more learning late into the evening. There was intense competition and pressure to earn the highest grades. Obtaining a good education was deeply ingrained in the minds of Koreans. We all felt that our life's success depended upon it!

In Mr. and Mrs. D's house, we had a bathroom inside of the house and both hot and cold running water. The soft toilet paper was so much better than newspaper or leaves. I could actually sit on a toilet seat and not squat!

My mom and I used to go to a pubic bathhouse in preparation for the New Year celebration. We used to soak our bodies with many other ladies in a big hot tub. When we got really warm, we would use small hand towels to exfoliate our skin. I would rub my mom's back and she mine. But when the weather was warm, we bathed ourselves by the creek. Men would also bathe themselves by the creek, but the ladies would walk a little farther up the creek from the men. When I was bathing by the creek, I always loved to sit under the waterfalls and let the water slide down my back. Tonight, at Mrs. D's house, I could take a warm bath all by myself. I lay in the tub singing songs and thinking of the weekend when I could see my mom again.

Chapter Nine

Dream & The Reservoir

When I went to my new enclosed porch bedroom, Mrs. D's cleaning lady and cook was already on the top bunk. She said, "Good night, Sooni." I replied in the same, considerate manner while wishing her to sleep well! It must have worked well because she was asleep quickly. I lay still at the bottom of the bunk bed, listening to her breathing. The warm bath made me feel comfortable and relaxed enough to become quite drowsy.

Sleep followed, but instead of comfort and peace, I cried out in my sleep. I was weeping and crying aloud. Tears were soaking my face, I was holding my mom's body, limp and cold on my lap. Tears and sweat drenched my covers. My crying became a wail which awoke me. I woke up sobbing, my arms wrapped around myself, crying like I had never cried before. I had experienced the most earth-shattering nightmare imaginable. Mrs. Kim called to me from the top bunk. "What is the matter, Sooni? What is the matter?" "It was so real," I blurted out with tears still streaming from my face. "I was hugging Umma's dead body. I was hugging Umma's dead body! My dream! My dream was so real. It was so terrible." Mrs. Kim tried to comfort me and said, "We can all have terrible dreams sometimes. Now try to get some sleep." But as I lay in bed, I kept wondering where such a nightmare could come from. Was it a sign of things to come?

I looked for the moon through the glass porch wall. Is Umma looking at the same moon and thinking of me now as I am thinking of her? My spirit became quiet and calm as I breathed slow and deep. I am alive. It was a dream. Just a bad dream. I was glad to have the peace to sleep and thankful that Mrs. Kim was on the top bunk. She cared enough to be my Auntie tonight. I coaxed myself to sleep. I can't be too tired for school. The rooster will soon be crowing in Umma's town, Pubwon-ni.

It had been several days since my bad dream. Although I tried to block it out of my mind, it came back and visited me often. Why did I have such a bad dream? One late Spring morning, I was about to begin my second block Math class. The bell had just rung to begin my favorite class of the day. All the students were obediently seated, as always. There was a knock at the classroom door. My Principal wanted to see me. I thought about something I could have done wrong for him to want to see me, but could not come up with anything. My heart was sinking. Why did he want to talk to me?

I could not believe what the principal gave me to read. I was incredulous. The telegram said, "Goo Sooni's mother died. Her body was found by the reservoir yesterday." Am I still dreaming? Oh, please let me still be dreaming! This couldn't possibly be true. She is the only person I have in the world. "God, you cannot take her away from me! No. No, you can't. I need her so!" I kept telling myself that it was a dream, and when I awoke all would be well. But it was not a dream. I couldn't even cry. I was choking up and gasping for air. I felt like I couldn't even breathe. After I was excused from school, I remember running from the school to my social worker, Miss Moon's house. It was close to the school. I was so glad she was so close to school!

Miss Moon was not home but her mother was there. She attempted to comfort me. She gave me some money and I went to the bus station. I knew this station well. I often went to Pubwon-ni to see my mom from here. I ran so fast I barely noticed my surroundings. I asked the bus driver, "Is this the bus to Pubwon-ni?" After giving him some won, I found a seat and stared straight through the window.

My mind felt numb but my heart cried, filled with grief and fear. "How can this be? The last time I saw her she wanted me to stay with her longer. Oh, how I wish I had stayed with Umma! Maybe then she would not have died. Was she so lonely? Or, did she think that if she wasn't around, Mr. and Mrs. D might adopt me or PSB Opportunity Center might make it possible for me to go to America? But didn't she let me go through all the adoption procedures with another American couple when I was little, but kidnapped me back later? Umma, you said you couldn't live without me. How could you be apart from me now, Umma?" As I looked out the window, the only thing I saw was Umma's face. Her lovely smile, the twinkle in her eyes as she stared at me. She was always there for me. She gave all she had and sacrificed so much to provide for me. It is only because of her that I am at school getting an education. Because of her dream, I am not in a ditch forever. "How can I live without you? Ummaaaaa.......!"

The bus driver called out, "Pubwon-ni Station!" I felt as though I was walking in a dream. I nodded to thank the driver. He nodded back. Neither of us smiled. I think he could tell something was wrong.

I walked to the police station. I reported myself to a policeman. "I am Goo Sooni. I brought this telegram you sent me." "I know you, Sooni," the policeman said. "Let's go for a walk. After walking for a while, I wondered if we were going to the reservoir. I knew this path well. My mom and I often came here on the way to the Buddhist temple. I could see the pagoda where people rested by the reservoir.

There was a man by himself fishing in a small boat. But the policeman guided me down on a stony path. The stones were wet from the shallow flowing of water. On the edge, I could see a large bundle covered with a straw mat and a man standing close by. Everything in me urged me to run away, but something still kept me walking. When I came near the bundle, I saw a body in a stretcher covered with the straw mat. I could see Umma's bloated body. I desperately wanted to touch her, to hug her just one more time. I was not able to save her. "Can this be real? Is this Umma?" I grieved so deep inside of my body, but I could not even cry. I so wanted to hold Umma just as it was in my dream many days ago. The smell of her body drove me away. Her body was green against her white Korean dress.

The policeman asked, "Is this your Umma?" I nodded. "How do you know?" "This looks like her face, and this is her dress." "Is her name Jung Song Ja?" I nodded. "Someone reported her missing," the policeman said. The other man said, "A fisherman saw her jump three days ago. "Jump?" They nodded and pointed to the pagoda balcony.

"She climbed over the railing and jumped. The fisherman rowed his boat to the spot where her body disappeared, but he was not able to find her. She was found last evening." "Where can I bury her?"

“We have a plot for her,” the policeman said. He and the other man carried the stretcher bearing Umma’s stiff body. When we arrived at the plot, there were already shovels there for us. I knew even from childhood that this was not a respectable burial ground. This was a ‘no man’s land.’ On one side of the hill, there was a huge chasm caused by the monsoon. This was a place unfit for burying anyone. But I had no choice. I thought they had disrespected Umma for what she had done for a living. The policemen did not understand that she did it to survive and keep me alive.

The policeman said, “I need to get back to the office. This man will help you.” We proceeded to dig a hole to bury Umma’s body. We put a cloth the man had brought along over the straw mat that had covered Umma’s body. As I was tucking the cloth around the stretcher, the man took another long sip of alcohol. We piled rocks over her to protect her body from the wild animals. Then we kept throwing the dirt over her. Scraping dirt from the side of the hill, we made a mound.

If Aunt Sughil, Halmauni, and Aunties knew about this burial, they would have been here. I was alone at the grave other than this man helping me. I felt numb. What has just happened? How I wanted this to be a dream! “Oh God, where are you?”

I was emotionally, physically, and mentally empty. I fell into the bus seat to return to Seoul, to Mr. and Mrs. D’s house. When I arrived, I found out that they had already been told about Umma’s death and where I was. However, they had no idea that I had to bury my own mother. The following Sunday, Mr. and Mrs. D offered to take me to Umma’s house in Pubwon-ni to gather her things. I was so thankful they offered to do this with me. As hard as the burial was, this would have been more difficult to do alone. Some Aunties took a few of my Umma’s belongings and I took Umma’s ever-present scarf. The only really nice thing my mom had was the rice container that had already been given to Mrs. D for taking care of me. I hugged each of the Aunties so tightly.

They said to me, “You are a rose, a beautiful rose. You will always live in our hearts.”

“Good-bye. I love you, Aunties. Please say ‘Good-bye’ to Halmauni.”

Then we drove to the reservoir. Mr. D parked his car by the bottom of the hill and we walked up to where my mother’s grave was. The trauma of Umma’s death overwhelmed me. While Mrs. D was holding onto me, Mr. D took a picture of my mom’s grave. Besides Mr. and Mrs. D opening their home to me, I was deeply grateful to have the few pictures of my mom and me and the grave. Even though it was not a respectable burial ground, it was where my Umma’s body lay. “Rest in peace, Umma. You will always live in my heart.”

Umma’s rounded grave mound at right.

Chapter Ten

Pearl S. Buck Opportunity Center

The next day, when I came out of my Han Yang Dae Huk Go Middle School, Miss Moon was waiting for me. She gave me such a heartfelt hug, and her expression of care and concern was indescribable. After a little conversation, Miss Moon said, "Sooni, would you like to come and live at the Pearl S. Buck Opportunity Center in Sosa?" I asked her, "What about Mr. and Mrs. D's? "They already know and would be fine with you going there." After only five months, I was moving again.

I never seemed to stay in one place for too long. I respected Miss Moon's opinion that my going to the Pearl S. Buck Opportunity Center would be a good decision for me. I did not fully understand why I said, "Yes" to the move but I knew I needed to trust the wisdom of a group of adults who really cared for me. And, in the wake of Umma's death, her dream of me going to America, the land of my father's birth, seemed more achievable with this next move.

When I arrived at the Pearl S. Buck Foundation's Opportunity Center, sometime in May of 1967, I was greeted by the director, Mr. Amos. "So, this is Sooni?" he said with a warm and caring smile. My smile back at him confirmed my answer. After spending some time in Miss Moon's office, I was taken to the girls' dormitory. It stood next to an equally large boys' dormitory. Both building were once factories, and now they housed all the young people at the PSB Opportunity Center – students who would also become friends.

We also saw the cafeteria where my days of extreme hunger would become a distant, but still real memory. I never wanted to be hungry again! Next to the cafeteria was the home of Mr. and Mrs. Amos and their children. There was also a beautiful open field covered with plush grass. I wanted to take my shoes off and run on it but decided to save that joy for later. I had never seen as many children who looked like me – half-Korean and half-American. I felt I was one of them. Being born at the end of the Korean War, I was one of the oldest of the Amerasians. I so enjoyed caring for the younger kids who seemed to welcome my presence in their lives. I belonged and was accepted among other children, something that was new to me. At Pearl Buck's Opportunity Center, I was no longer, "Tigi – a yankee devil."

Living at the Opportunity Center and commuting to my Hang Yang Dae Huk Go Middle School was now a much longer commute than I had before. I needed to walk to the train station at around 5:30 AM. After about a forty-minute train ride, I would walk out of the train terminal and to a bus stop. My bus ride was about twenty minutes. After another ten- minute walk, I arrived at the school gate. With all the waits in between, I arrived at school at around 7:45. This routine was followed six school days a week – Monday through Saturday – two hours to school and two hours home to the dormitory.

The train became a good place to study. It was spacious and quiet. The bus ride, however, was crowded and it felt as though I was in a packed sardine can. Every day, the bus attendant would push and shove us to squeeze more people into the sardine can! We looked like an Egyptian painting with arms and legs pointing in different directions.

The ladies in Western clothing were concerned that the school bags of the students like me would be catching onto their stockings. Each night when I got home to the dormitory, I needed to cover my sneakers in thick white chalk. My sneakers needed to be white when I entered the school gate, so I brushed the chalk, which served as a protectant while on the crowded bus. If my sneakers were dirty, the upper-class sisters would spank the palms of my hands for not having clean sneakers. Each classroom had about 70-80 students. The teacher would line us up by our height and seat us with the shortest in the front. I was #41. I guess that meant that my height was about average.

Although I was busy during the school day, with school work, homework, dormitory chores, and about four hours of travel – as I walked and waited for the train and busses in between, thoughts of Umma's death continued to overwhelm me. There were people around me but I felt all alone. There was not even a distant relative that I could call mine. I was truly an orphan. There was no way to contact any of my mom's relatives in North Korea, and even if they did know of me, they would disown me for being a half-breed, their sister bringing shame upon the family because of my existence. Fear grabbed my soul and yanked at my heart. What would become of me? "God," I cried, "I don't know who you are, but would you protect me and provide me with a family someday. I just want a home. I want someone to love me and have my love returned."

Perhaps with an education, I might find a future. I purposed in my heart to honor my mom's memory and study very hard. I studied while my new friends played and while they slept. In this big dormitory, we would have small bunk beds lined up in long rows. The lights went out by 10:00 each evening. I would study on my bed, which was quite low to the ground, and at 10:00 I would gather up my books, notebooks, and pencils and tiptoe into the bathroom, my late-night study room! When I got sleepy, I would slap my face and pinch my legs to keep myself awake and focused on my studying. Korean students are known for going to school after school to supplement their learning. The dormitory bathroom at 10:00 each evening became my school after school. I knew I needed to do better than my best. I was driven to honor my mother's life. She gave all of herself for me that I could live and not stay in the ditch.

When I did well in school, it gave me a sense of worth. And, that drove me to do better. I smiled as I thought of the times when Umma twirled me around the room, giggling and laughing when I brought a good paper home. Those thoughts lightened my heart. I wanted my Umma to be happy and proud of me even in her death. At the end of seventh grade in February, 1968, I received my report card. From a list posted near the office, I found out that I was ranked first in the class of more than 600 girls. My efforts did not go in vain. I certainly knew I was not the

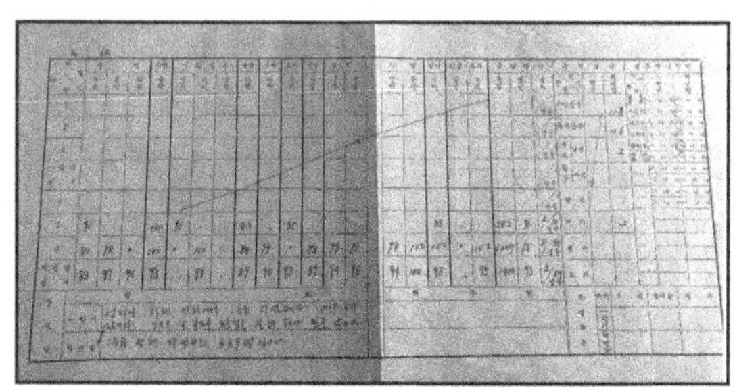

Julie's report card.

smartest in the class. I was scared, lonely, and hungry for an opportunity to rise above my Amerasian upbringing. I thought that with an education, I might have a better future. My heart drove me to study. I was so happy to show my report to Miss Moon. She was absolutely delighted, took me by the hand, and shared the good news with Mr. Amos. Mr. Amos said, "I am so proud of you, Sooni! I need to tell this to Pearl Buck." He then wrote a letter to Miss Buck in America, informing her of my top-class rank.

Early in the spring of 1968, Miss Buck came to the Pearl S. Buck Opportunity Center in Sosa, Korea. This was the lady who made it possible for me to have a place to stay, to study, and to go on with my life. I was so thankful that I had food to eat. I didn't have to wonder whether I would be able to get my next meal. I never liked how my body felt when I was so hungry.

I liked living in the Opportunity Center. They were all Amerasians, the name Miss Buck gave to children who had American fathers and Asian mothers. Within the boundary of this dormitory, no one teased or ridiculed us and we accepted each other for who we were. Besides our schooling, we were given opportunities to learn baking, tailoring, and haircutting. I chose to learn tailoring, and it was fun to measure, draw, cut, and sew.

I still went to my all-girls high school in Seoul. Although there was an elementary school nearby that went to the sixth grade, there was no school for my age. In the Winter, it would sometimes be dark by the time I arrived back at my dormitory at the Opportunity Center in Sosa.

Julie in foreground, Pearl S. Buck Opportunity Center in background.

Pearl S. Buck Opportunity Center with Amerasian children.

Junior High School - Julie is on the left.

Pearl S. Buck visiting the Sosa Opportunity Center

Chapter Eleven

Pearl S. Buck, My Final Duty, & America

The day came when Miss Moon came for me and said that Miss Buck wanted to meet me. I could not believe this famous American wanted to see me. How thrilled I was at the thought of actually meeting Miss Buck, the woman we all adored. My heart was pounding.

When I entered the office, she was seated in an armchair. Miss Buck was such a beautiful, dignified lady with striking silver hair and twinkling, deep blue eyes. She smiled at me and I shyly returned it. I felt the warmth in her smile. She asked me to come nearby to sit. Then, through an interpreter, she asked me if I would like to come to America to live with her as her daughter. I could not believe what I heard. I was so excited that I could have jumped to the top of the ceiling if I could. "I am going to America! I am going to America! God, I do not know who you are, I do not even know where you are, but I am thanking you so, so, very much for taking care of me."

Julie and Mother Pearl
Pearl S. Buck

The process of getting my visa to America was another story. I did not even have a birth certificate or any citizenship papers whatsoever. However, Miss Buck's political influence was significant and made it possible for me to get a visa to America. How did she do that? I do not know but was truly thankful!

It was fun going to many different places to get things ready to go to America. I was even measured by a tailor so I could have a dress and a jacket for the trip to my new home, America. It was a pretty, orange, sleeveless dress with a matching fitted jacket. I even got brand new shoes to match the outfit. I remember the cream-colored shoes with an orange stripe in the front and a purse that I could put around my shoulder. Never in my life had I been treated this well. I felt pretty in my new outfit and accessories.

So many of my friends from the PSB Opportunity Center were so happy for me. The thoughts of leaving my friends saddened my heart, but the desire to go to America was so strong, that my saddened heart did not last too long. One cannot imagine the thoughts that I had about the prospect of moving to America. I dreamed of what a wonderful place it must be. People lived well, had lots of food, clothes, cars, and many things to make life comfortable. The land of opportunity where one could be whatever he put his mind to be. This is the land where everyone is accepted despite one's color or creed. This is the best place in the whole wide world to live! My friends and I often dreamed of going there. And I was chosen to go. The thought of it was overwhelming. How can this be? "Umma, can you see from where you are what is about to happen to me? Oh, how I miss you!"

There was one more thing I needed to take care of before I went to America. In Korean culture, most of the "grave" is above the ground – a mound. When the plot is not taken care of – grass cut and weeds pulled, it can become a place where wild animals gather. Family care of the gravesite is a token of respect, love, and appreciation of the deceased. Many Koreans believed when people die, their spirit stays with their family for about four generations. For me to not take care of my mother's grave would be the worst thing I could ever do.

I spoke with Mr. Amos, the PSB Korea director, about what I needed to do. He said that he would come with me. I told him, I needed to do this for my mom myself. Mr. Amos was such a caring man to me and all of us at the center. He respected what I needed to do. He gave me

$50 of his own money. I so gratefully accepted his gift. I went to my hometown, Pubwon-ni, and walked up to the Buddhist Temple.

I used to walk up this winding way to the temple with my mom! I remember her carrying me on her back when I got too tired. I could never get used to the pictures of the gods. They always looked so scary and made me want to try and behave myself. I also didn't enjoy bowing to the Buddha statue 108 times all the way down to the floor and up again and again. It made my head dizzy but I had wanted to please my mom and not anger Buddha.

When I arrived at the temple, one of the Buddhists knew my name. He and another monk walked with me to my mother's grave. Many months had passed since my mother's death. The monks exhumed my mother's body which was covered in a straw mat. The three of us took my mother's body back to the temple where it was cremated. Then, late in the afternoon, the monk presented my mother's remains to me in an urn. I thanked them for their service and help and gave them the money Mr. Amos had given to me.

I boarded a bus to Seoul, and sprinkled my mother's ashes into the Han River. My mother had told me how she used to cross the bridge from where I cast the ashes and the urn. "Umma, rest well. May your spirit be in peace knowing how much I love you." I then walked to the train station, rode back to Sosa, and made the long walk to the Opportunity Center. It was a clear, cool night and the moon was as round as a saucer. I was wearing my Hanbok that day to honor my mother and her ancestors.

All that had happened that day came over me. It was quite a day for a fourteen-year-old child of mixed race, all alone in a land that was not fully her home. Walking to the dormitory, I was scared even of my own shadow. "Umma, why did you take your own life? You talked of how you wanted me to go to America, but you would not let me go when a couple from America wanted to adopt me. Were you thinking, since I am older now, who would want me? Were you thinking that if you took yourself out of the picture, the PSB Foundation would take care of me better? Umma, why? I love you so much. Oh, how I miss you!"

The day I had been eagerly awaiting finally arrived – Thursday, May 30, 1968. This was the first airplane I had ever seen except from a book. Now, I was in one. How exciting the plane ride was! I could see the landforms of Korea while up in the air. As the country "shaped like a rabbit" faded behind me, I said good-bye to Korea. "I do not know when I will see you again. Be well, land of my mother."

The airplane stopped in Japan for almost five hours. I got out of the plane but I didn't want to walk too far away from the gate for fear of getting lost. I enjoyed looking at the twinkling lights of stores. There were so many pretty things in the shops. The beautiful ladies on the airplane fed me well. The food was so good! I enjoyed the pretzels and peanuts. When I got chilly and tired, the pretty lady brought me a pillow and a warm blanket. How can she be so caring and kind? I kept showing my gratitude by saying, "I preciate." She smiled at my attempt to thank her. Could I ever have a job like hers someday? I would then also be nice to others and offer my help with a smile as this lady had for me. After twenty-two hours of traveling including another stopover in Seattle, I finally arrived at Philadelphia International Airport at around 2:00 AM. I had left Seoul on a Thursday, and after being in the air for 22 hours, it was still Thursday in Philadelphia!

Miss Buck was at the airport to greet me. I couldn't believe I was standing on American soil! I was not able to put on my new shoes since my feet had swollen up so much during the flight. I should have kept my shoes on my feet the entire trip from Seoul. I was so used to being in bare feet. In agony, I pushed my swollen feet into dress shoes I was unaccustomed to wearing. That did not last too long. I walked through the airport in bare feet and carried my shoes. I remember the tender smile on Miss Buck's face as she looked at her new "daughter" carrying her shoes. I smiled back.

We were soon all in a big black car. The driver was a big and tall man. I don't remember ever seeing such a big man in my entire life. He did not say much, but I could see a gentleness about his smile. I was quiet as well. I was quite tired and was afraid to say anything.

Chapter Twelve

Green Hills Farm

We went through a long tunnel in Philadelphia. I had never been through such a tunnel before. My mind was very uneasy until we came out of it. It seemed to go on and on with the bright lights on my face. I felt I needed to hold my breath. After a bit more than an hour, we finally arrived at Miss Buck's farmhouse. My heart was pounding as we entered the gate and drove up the long driveway. I could see trees everywhere! Can this possibly be my new home? It was very foggy that night. Through the hazy mist, I could see a wonderland of trees and a pond with lights from the house sparkling across its surface.

Entering the house, I first remember the huge red kitchen countertop, a big table in the middle of the kitchen, and an adorable black pot stove on a wall. In the dining room were the most beautiful blue and white draperies on iron rods and a reddish stone floor that was cold to the touch of my bare feet.

Sketch of kitchen pot stove by Julie Henning

Exiting the dining room, there were beautiful orange drapes on each side of the doorway as we entered the living room. This room had many large, thick wooden beams across the ceiling. I remember thinking – "Why didn't she cover the wooden beams with wallpaper as the Korean people did? Only poor people in Korea don't cover their ceilings with paper. Maybe Miss Buck was poor, too. I soon was shown to my bedroom where I could not believe what I saw. I had my own

Acrylic Painting of Green Hills Farm by Julie Henning.

bathroom along with a fireplace in my room and a balcony I could access. I even had my own bed – and it was more than a mattress on the floor. I knew I should be going to bed, but the excitement and the height of my new bed placed a fear in me to go to sleep – I might fall out of my bed! I finally dragged the blanket, comforter, and my pillow down to the spotless bedroom floor and promptly fell asleep. It felt so good to wiggle my toes under the blanket. This is now my room. In my entire fourteen years on this earth, I had never before fallen asleep in my own room, except for my few weeks at Mr. and Mrs. D's house.

The next morning as I entered the kitchen, a wonderful aroma greeted me. Soon I found it was called "bacon." Seated at a large wooden table that took up much of the room, I also had some eggs, whole wheat toast covered with honey. It was fun to scoop the honey from the bee's wax. And the taste of freshly squeezed orange juice was delectable. How could so many oranges cut in half make so little orange juice? The sunshine warmed the kitchen as its brightness shown through the large kitchen window. Sitting in her chair at the table, Miss Pearl Buck looked so lovely in her pretty grey top. It showed off her silvery hair and her beautiful blue eyes. Her warm welcome made my heart warmer with gratitude and joy. "You may call me Mother," she said. Then I smiled and said, "You are my new mother."

As I looked around each room of my new home in the daylight, I was amazed at the grace and beauty and the warmth of the house – not to mention all the books mother had in her two big libraries. Even more books were in her office. Books seemed to cover the walls of almost every room in the house! The wide wooden steps with pocket doors led to the biggest library just off the living room. The east side of the library was all glass walls, looking out to the courtyard. The courtyard was covered with brown, beige, orange, and some bluish looking stones. I could see the water fountain with a stone cupid on it. Watching the waterfall seemed to calm my somewhat anxious thoughts of the sudden, new normal of my life.

Out of the window of the smaller library, I could see a swing on a huge walnut tree. I ran out of the room and I sat on that swing. Oh, how I used to love to swing in Korea. On a swing I can fly, my thoughts can fly to any place I want them to go. It would soon become one of my very special places. I saw a swimming pool as I continued to walk through a long breezeway towards Mother's office.

Behind her desk, I saw two beautiful greenhouses. One was to grow flowers to be cut for décor throughout the house. The other greenhouse had hundreds of camellias beautifully bursting with colors of pink, rose and white. Mother told me how they were her favorite flowers when she was growing up in China. What a wonderful reminder they must have been of her childhood. I liked the double rows of a rose garden by the large, in-ground pool. When Mother sat in her chair at her typewriter, she could see her roses. I soon learned the love that mother had for her flowers, especially roses. Her bathroom color was rose, and most of the fabrics in her bedroom had rose patterns on them. Miss Buck's mother had also loved roses – a daughter like her mother. She would often cut fresh flowers and arrange them so nicely, not just on the top of her Steinway piano but all through the house and especially in her bedroom. I liked the way she decorated. Her arrangements consisted of just a few flowers placed with balance and elegance. Mother received so much joy and contentment from her work with flowers.

The more I looked around, the more there was to see! Miss Buck had so much land along with her beautiful farmhouse. She owned more than 500 acres. The landscaping was well kept by two men, Mr. Galla and his son, who faithfully and carefully maintained the property. It seems like the lawn was so large that they had to continually cut the grass with the tractor to just keep up with the lawn's growth. They did such a wonderful job and I so enjoyed running around on the open fields.

Photo of Green Hills Farm today.

Mrs. Galla kept the inside of the house arranged and spotless. The big, wide wooden floorboards were so shiny, I could almost see the reflection of my face. Mrs. Galla even cleaned my bedroom. I liked the lemony scent pouring from my room after she had cleaned it.

The only thing I had to do was wash my own clothes. And, in America, I did not have to go to the distant creek and rub my clothes against a stone to clean them. I remember the sound of the flowing stream and my Umma washing next to me, working so diligently. Now, in my new home in America, I have a washing machine that does the wash on its own and a dryer in the mud room that dries my clothes so fluffy and nice. Also, in the middle of the mud room with its red brick floor, there was even a hand pump and drain. I didn't have to go outside to clean off my muddy shoes. I had no worries about the rain, snow, or being cold.

The neatest thing about the mud room was when I opened the small closet door on the wall, an ironing board popped out! I never saw anything so clever. After ironing, I could hide it back in the wall. Ironing clothes became a labor of love. Before I went to the happy orphanage in Korea, I had only one outfit to wear. When it got dirty, Umma would have to wash it by the well at night, while I was huddled up in a blanket hoping that my clothes would dry by the next morning. I had no other clothes to wear to school. Some cold mornings I imagined "steam" coming off my body – only to learn later that it was condensation from my clothes that had not fully dried overnight.

Because of the generosity of my new mother, I was allowed to go to the nice stores in Doylestown. Mr. Ottinger, Mother's chauffeur, would drive me there and I would pick out the items that I needed or sometimes just wanted. I only had to sign my new name, "Julie Walsh," and Mother would pay it all. I was so humbled and honored to bear her name. It was so wonderful to have a mother again. I longed for a mother since my loving Umma died, and now I had a mother in Miss Buck.

Julie by fountain
at Green Hills Farm
in 1968

Julie by fountain
at Green Hills Farm
in 2014

Julie indicating
brick in honor and
memory of
Mother Pearl
on brick walkway
at Green Hills Farm

Vintage picture of the Red Barn as viewed from the front.

Current day rear view of the former Red Barn, now transformed into PSBI's Cultural Center, with the spring house to the right.

Chapter Thirteen

New Mother, New School

"Good morning, Mother!" I joyfully said when I kissed her on her cheek or on her forehead as she was seated at the breakfast table. That became our morning ritual – a delightful expression of security as we sat down to enjoy a delicious breakfast together.

Mrs. Loris reminded me of my Halmauni from Korea. I soon found out she hardly ever missed coming to cook for Mother. She had the sweetest smile, and I always appreciated Mrs. Loris's fresh-squeezed orange juice every morning. The noise of the juicer was a sure sign of coming refreshment. Mother's bacon and scrapple were so well done that the crunchiness was heard as she ate. She also liked her eggs prepared in a very unusual way. They were scrambled with a touch of soy sauce and tabasco sauce for a tangy, spicy taste.

Mother liked lots of spiced food, including Kimchee, a Korean cabbage seasoned with chili powder, scallions, garlic, ginger, and salted seafood. In Korea, when my Umma made it, she would store the kimchee underground in jars to keep it cool and unfrozen during the winter months. Now, Mother would be pleased when I made the dish, but she would be teasingly frustrated when she had a speaking engagement and knew she should not be touching kimchee because of the strong garlic breath it produced!

Mother enjoyed sweets as much as she relished spicy foods. Having grown up in a culture where we were too poor to ever have sweets, Mother quickly convinced me that a bowl of ice cream topped off with Kellogg's Sugar Frosted Flakes and genuine maple syrup was a treat beyond my wildest dreams! One night, I heard some noises in the kitchen and decided to find out what it was. There was Mother eating her delightful dessert. Her blue eyes said she was surprised to see me, and she smiled as I made a bowl for myself. We had a great time laughing and enjoying our sneaky treats together.

One morning, Mrs. Shaddinger, Mother's secretary, was making a grocery list and I told her what kind of ice cream I liked – 'vanilla and rum raisin.' We had a huge, walk-in freezer, about the size of my one-room Korean house. It was located in the barn next to Miss Buck's house. All different flavors of ice cream were there. The containers were shaped like cylinders. When I first tasted ice cream at the age of fourteen, I really thought I was in heaven. I would first have ice cream around ten o'clock in the morning, then after lunch, after a swim, for dessert at suppertime, and before going to bed. Before I knew it, Mr. Galla said, "Julie, you are turning into a Crisco can!" I was on a "see food" diet. Whatever I saw, I ate. After so many years of not knowing if I would have a next meal, I had to re-program my brain that there would be food tomorrow.

My Korean half-sister had died of malnutrition before she reached age two. My Umma vowed not to lose another. She put me into different orphanages as I was growing up so I would be regularly fed in the winter. When she was able to get enough food for me to come home, she would return to the orphanage and take me away. This went on for many years. I can still hear her say, "Soonyia, when you look at the moon, I will be looking at the same moon and thinking of you." I also knew that Umma would always come for me.

Now, with food whenever I wanted it, I realized that eating too much could also make me fat! In Korea, I ate when we had food and went hungry when we had no food. In Korea, I was never concerned about my weight or eating too many calories. I could remember the pangs in my stomach when I was so hungry and longing for food. Believe it or not, until I arrived at the PSBI dormitory at age 13, I had never used a toothbrush. I had cleaned my teeth with my index finger dabbed with salt and yet never had a cavity. Within months of having a toothbrush and discovering ice cream in Mother's barn, I got my first tooth cavity filled!

One day, Mrs. Robinson came to our house. She informed me that she was to be my English tutor. Mother asked her to prepare me for the local public school that I would be starting in September. Mrs. Robinson was very pretty and nice. Her kind voice made me feel safe and comfortable. Most importantly, she was patient with me as I struggled to learn the English language. We looked at lots of pictures with words beneath them. She would point to the words and say what the picture was. I would then try to repeat what she said. We also learned about sentence structure, but the ideas were so hard to understand.

Once, as I was studying in the kitchen, Mother said to me, "Turn out the light before you go to bed." I was puzzled. Why should I put the light bulb and the light outside? When I told that story to Mrs. Robinson, she laughed and laughed. From that first experience, idioms were (and are) a major struggle. As I was diligently working on learning my new language, my nighttime dreams became a fascination. Some of my dreams were in Korean and others were in English. I remember the clarity in my English dreams was better than my speaking skills. Mother also said, "Julie, try to watch at least one hour of television each evening." She wanted me to see some of the American ways while hearing the language spoken. It was a drain to try to watch for an entire hour without understanding much of anything coming from the box in front of me. Nevertheless, I watched as Mother had asked. Slowly, I found myself recognizing and understanding more and more of the words being spoken.

In the Summer of 1968, I prepared as much as I knew how before entering Pennridge South Junior high as a ninth grader in September. I remember there was some discussion as to whether I would enter eighth or ninth grades. I remember that after being at the Happy Orphanage, I stayed home for nine months, not being able to afford to go to school. I did go to school for about two months of eighth grade in Korea before I came to America. Since I did not know the language well enough, it did not really matter which grade I entered. Since it was just as easy to not know English in ninth grade as it was in eighth grade, I was placed in the higher grade. Mr. Ottinger picked me up from school in mother's limousine and drove me to Mrs. Robinson's house several days after school, where she tutored me in English. However, I always preferred riding in the big yellow school bus. I just liked the cute American boys!

I could not speak English too well in ninth grade, but my classmates seemed to accept me and tried to understand what I attempted to say. A smile became my stand-by. Whenever I could not understand what was being said, I shrugged my shoulders and smiled. Sometimes, my classmates would talk very s-l-o-w or louder to me, thinking that the slowness or volume would help me to better understand what they were saying. I sometimes shed many silent tears due to my frustration in the classroom. Not only could I not understand much of what was being said but, when I could understand, I was mostly unable to express what I knew, nor could I ask questions about what I did not know.

My experience in Korea was a constant reminder that I was not stupid, but I was extremely frustrated with my lack of adjustment to education in America with a new language. I began to copy any English word I saw on the chalkboard. I found all those words in my English-Korean dictionary. When I saw the English words next to the Korean words, I could try to make sense of the concepts that were taught that day. Math was easier for me since numbers are a universal language. I studied and studied and somehow, I got onto the honor roll for the first marking period. I really did not understand or learn much but I was able to give the correct answers from all the memory work I did. Truthfully, I believe the teachers were a bit easier on my work, realizing the limitation of my English. Sometimes I studied so hard at home that I would make an ice pack to stay awake and study more at night. Something in me drove my passion to study. It gave me great pleasure to see the delightful look on my new mother's face when she saw that I was understanding my school work.

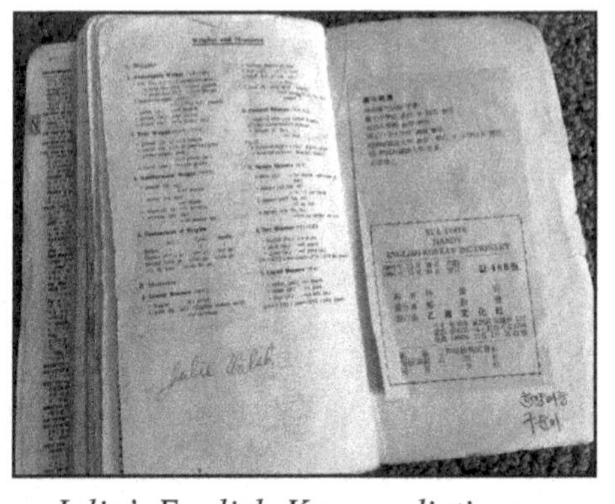

Julie's English-Korean dictionary

"Umma, I am in America as you hoped for me. I miss you and think of you every day. I will continue to study hard, Umma."

Once I was given an opportunity to present the Korean culture and its people before an assembly of my fellow students and our teachers at my junior high. I spoke about some of the Korean customs, education,

My Junior high teacher Yi Yin Soon

food, and clothing styles in my broken English. And I ended the assembly by doing a Korean folk dance using a pretty fan and wearing my Hanbok. This was a beautiful Hanbok which Yi Yin Soon, my math teacher in Korea, had given to me before I left for America. She was so good to me. She had lost her son at about the time Umma died. We understood each other's pain even without speaking many words. My Pennridge schoolmates seemed to enjoy the program and were curious about my Korean heritage.

I continued to make friends and my fifteenth birthday party was such a grand one for me! I had never had a birthday party before. In our big library, Mother installed a record player on the wall in the closet beneath the large library's staircase. The outside of the door looked just like part of the wall, but when opened, the record player appeared, playing both 33 and 45 rpm records. With music playing, I enjoyed dancing with my friends and celebrating my first American birthday. In this room, because of its tall glass doors, I could see the reflections of my friends also enjoying themselves. As with the "record player in the wall," Mother always had a way of making things useful, practical, and yet beautiful.

Julie standing next to her Hanbok now on display at Green Hills Farm

That is around the time I met my friend, Jeff. He was kind and had a good sense of humor. He helped me with my English. He often did not have much to say, but it was easy for us to spend time on the phone each day after school giggling through our conversations. He would often try to explain things during my silent moments and he would laugh at my pronunciations. It was good to have a friend. Judy was my very special friend. She often came over to my house and we loved walking around the fields. I think she was taken aback when I held her hand. In Korea, girlfriends often walk hand-in-hand. I learned that in America, they do not.

Soon after I came to America, I met two new sisters who were about to be married. Henrietta Walsh was an adopted daughter of Pearl Buck and her husband Richard Walsh. Henrietta's elegant wedding was held at our Green Hills farmhouse. So many people were there. I remember thinking how beautiful Henrietta looked!

I dreamed that someday, I would be married there, too. I already chose a perfect spot, at the edge of the lawn. There was a long row of trees growing on either side of a wide part of the field. At the end of the trees there was a small pond with a stone, cupid fountain. I remember thinking that this would be the perfect spot for me to have a wedding someday.

The reception's hors d'oeuvres and champagne were served on the lawn. I remember that I tasted my first champagne that day. I do not remember especially liking the taste, but I thought it was a neat idea and I drank more than I should have. The next day, I had an awful headache. Why do people drink if it gives them headaches afterwards? Why did I drink? A second wedding followed a just few months later. This time it was Cheiko Walsh's turn. Her wedding was very different from Henrietta's. Cheiko wanted a very simple event. She even made her own wedding dress. Maybe she just ran out of time, but I remember her sewing the finishing touches on her dress close to the time she was to put it on to walk down the aisle. These two weddings at Miss Buck's farmhouse, when I was fifteen and so soon after I had arrived, were both beautiful, but uniquely different.

A few days after the weddings and we were alone in a much quieter house, Mother said, "Julie, have you ever taken piano lessons before?" I smiled and said, "No." "The piano is a lovely instrument. Would you like to learn how to play?" I replied, "Yes, please!" Mother then arranged for a piano tutor to come to our house. I was very excited in the beginning but soon found out that I did not like to practice playing the piano. My lessons were on Tuesdays, and Tuesdays came way too fast! But I was to take at least one year of piano lessons. After the year was over, to my later regret, I stopped. That was a decision I wish I had not been allowed to make for myself.

Music was a very important part of Mother's life. She played the piano and organ very well. I loved listening to her play. Mother also found great delight in listening to music. Once a month, we went to hear Eugene Ormandy conducting the Philadelphia Symphony Orchestra. I enjoyed the old classic performances, but modern performances usually caused me to fall asleep.

The best part about going to the orchestra was holding Mother's hand and walking into her special box seat on the second floor. Many people would stand up and wave to her. That was a special honor for Mother. I felt so privileged to be seated right next to her. I was just over five feet tall, but felt double that height, as I swelled with pride for my new Mother.

As we prepared to go to one performance, Mother and I were sitting in the limousine waiting for our driver, Mr. Ottinger, who was eating a snack in the kitchen. "Julie, would you let Mr. Ottinger know that we are ready to leave?" I replied, "Yes, Mother," then went to go look for him. As I was getting out of the car, my hand would not follow me! I had closed the car door with my thumb stuck in the door! Needless to say, we did not go to Philadelphia that night. The doctor had to take my thumb nail out and sew in quite a few stitches. "I am so sorry that we didn't go to the concert tonight," I said. "Don't put a second thought to it. You just take care of that thumb. I love you," she said. "I love you, too, Mother." I never realized how much I used my right thumb in the course of a day. The doctor instructed me to keep my thumb up by putting a sling around my shoulder for four weeks. When my thumb was not kept up, it throbbed more!

Dancing was another thing I was taught. Mother's dancing instructor was an Arthur Murray Studio Instructor, who had reddish hair and was always very well dressed. He taught me the waltz, the chachacha, and many other modern dance steps. He was a terrific dancer. When he would dance with me, he would make even a poor dance partner like me feel like I had some talent.

Her dance instructor invited us to go on a boat ride in Boston. The boat seemed like a living room on the water. I wore sunglasses for the first time. I felt like a movie star that day. In the evening, we went to a very nice seafood restaurant in Boston where Mother and all of us enjoyed a lobster dinner. It was so good! The waiter brought us a bib to wear while eating the lobster. I felt much too big to wear a bib but put it on along with everyone else. When the lemon bowl was brought out after the meal, I proceeded to drink from it! I soon found out the lemon was intended to get the lobster and butter smell off our fingers!

Another evening when I was with some friends for dinner, my friend Tom cared enough to tell me more of the American ways of dining. He told me to cut just a few pieces of meat at a time, eat them, then cut some more. I should not cut all the meat at one time. When I was growing up in Korea, we didn't even have a knife at the table. All the meat was cut before it was served. That way, it was easier to eat with chopsticks. A girl friend at the table that night told me that in America, girls shave their legs. I was embarrassed to hear that, but grateful for the information. Then I glanced at my legs and saw what looked like skinny worms under my stockings. Lesson learned. I need to shave my legs in America. I was learning things for the first time that I thought others my age had known for years.

It was Christmas Eve and the tree was fully and beautifully decorated by the corner window in the Large Library. I knew there was a big box with my name on it. Somehow that night, I just could not fall asleep. It was going to be the very first time that I would get a real Christmas gift rather than an orange and a bottle of ketchup that I had received from a GI wearing, what I now know was a Santa's outfit, when I was still small in Korea. I remember how much I enjoyed eating that ketchup with one chopstick. I would put the chopstick into the ketchup jar, pull it out and lick it! I did that many, many times until the bottle was empty. My tummy hurt, but the sweetness that I experienced over and over again was so worth it.

Tonight, I needed to find out what was in that beautifully gift-wrapped box. I so quietly came down the stairs and so carefully opened the box. "Ah-h-h!!" It was a gorgeous salmon-colored angora sweater with blue trim. I carefully re-taped the box, put it right back where it had been found, tiptoed back to my room, closed the door, and fell asleep. When I awoke Christmas morning, it was not as joyous as it should have been. I learned that I should not have opened the box in the middle of the night to take a sneak peek.

Because our home and family were not considered typically American, Mother made it possible for me to visit a local family about once a month to learn how a more typical American family lived. The Mills Family generously opened their home to me. They had three children of their own and it thrilled my heart to be with them. They were such a wholesome family and their kindness towards me was overwhelming. Their mother would often iron the family's clothes in the basement and I just watched her. In that basement, I also was introduced to the Lawrence Welk Show. The ladies in the show could sing and dance so well and I loved the outfits they were wearing. I knew that America is such a wonderful place!

I liked learning and exploring all the new ways of America, my father's land. And I felt truly secure, comfortable, and loved. But Mother wasn't feeling too well and we began taking more extended trips to her mountain home in Danby, Vermont, to let her rest in a quieter environment. I enjoyed Danby in the summer time, too. I loved hiking and climbing the mountains. When people in town were talking about sighting a bear in the mountains, I wondered what I would do if I saw a bear on one of my explorations.

The mountain house was such a wonderful place to be. Though she was feeling ill, I could easily understand the peace and serenity that pulled Mother to Vermont. We would have pancakes in the morning with genuine Vermont maple syrup – the same syrup we used on our ice cream and frosted flakes dessert back at home. One morning, I ate seven pancakes! Mother went to Vermont a lot during this time, but I mostly stayed home to attend school.

When she would come back to Green Hills, her beautiful Bucks County, Pennsylvania 18th century farmhouse, we would have lunches together every day that I was not in school. Just the two of us would sit at the small luncheon table right by the large windows in the dining room and look out at our patio. It was our special time. I enjoyed listening to her, her ideas, the people she knew, or a story. In my mind, she was always writing a story as we spoke. She had the unique ability to take two or three stories and put them together to write a meaningful and thought-provoking story. Even today I can hear her two-fingered typing on her keyboard…and she wrote so many stories just using two fingers!

The chess board in the Large Library

After lunch, we made time for a game of chess. Mother felt this was a special strategic game of mental exercise. Mother had a chess set made of carved soap-stone. It was given to her by the Korean people as a gift. The shapes of the King and the Queen I studied and understood. They were so meticulously made. Their familiar Korean figures were comforting to behold. My Korean elementary school had been filled with portraits of previous generations in the hallways. Though I could never get past the simple elements of chess, it was so good to spend time with Mother and learn from her. While I tried to prevent all the moves she could make, there always seemed to be one more – check-mate! The moves of chess enhanced my love for mathematics. Mother said I was becoming quite good at the game, but I only managed to beat her once. Truth be told, I think she allowed me to win so I would know the experience of victory and not get too discouraged!

Julie's sketch of a willow tree outside Mother's office.

Mother also had a large office. Where she sat, she could see through the double window, her rose garden, the pool, a small pond, and a larger one down the slope. Many trees surrounded the more distant pond. It was such a picturesque view that Mother said, "When I look out this view, it reminds me of when I lived in China." On a hazy or rainy day, the view from her office window looked like a beautiful painting. How disciplined she was to stay at work at her typewriter with such beauty surrounding her. I remember thinking how the beauty around her farm was such an inspiration for her writing.

In her office, she had a collection of stamps from many different countries. They came from her correspondence with so many people from all over the world. Mother would often say at breakfast, "Julie, I have more stamps for you." I eagerly went to office to receive the stamps she had that day for me. Placing the stamps in albums and studying the stamps gave me a love of stamp collecting. I enjoyed their unique designs.

Julie's stamp album

Something that I enjoyed so much were the times that mother would take me with her when she spoke and gave lectures at different colleges or at social functions. I remember feeling so proud of her! I saw Mother being honored by many but she seemed to lack close friendships. Most were in awe of her but may have felt that she was unapproachable as a friend. Mother realized that being famous had set her apart from others. I often wondered if she was sometimes lonely.

I remember one sunny day, when Mother was working in the rose garden by the pool. When Mother worked with flowers, she did not have to think – just enjoy the pleasure of the moment. Mr. Galla always did a wonderful job of maintaining the entire exterior of the home, but Mother still wanted to have a part in taking care of it. When I later stopped by her bedroom, mother looked as though she were about to fall asleep while reading a science magazine. She put the magazine aside and asked me to sit down. Mother was sitting on her rose-patterned chair with her feet propped up by a matching ottoman. My typical comfortable position was to sit on the floor facing her with my legs crossed in a lotus shape. I asked her, "May I sketch your legs?" She smiled and said, "Yes."

While I was sketching, I asked about her childhood. She told me how she was taken to China when she was three months old after having been born in West Virginia, the home of her mother's family. Mother's parents were missionaries to China and they were home on furlough when she was born.

She grew up among the Chinese people. Some of the other missionaries lived in a missionary compound, but her parents wanted to live side-by-side among the Chinese people. She played with Chinese children talking and listening to their ideas and their ways. She said, "I think I was better for having done that." Mother was schooled by her mother, who she referred to as Carie. Carie made sure Mother wrote something each week. Carie taught her English, reading, writing, and American culture.

Young Pearl also had a Chinese tutor who taught her Chinese reading and writing, history, and Confucianism. Mother explained to me, "Confucianism was a philosophy of living a simple way of life." Mother told me how proud she was when her first writing was published in a children's edition of the English language newspaper, *The Shanghai Mercury*. "I was even paid for the article, a fact that is still a great source of pride for me," Mother said.

One of Mother's most favorite things to do as a child was to read through her family's collection of Charles Dickens, especially *Oliver Twist*. I think she said she had read through them seven times. To this day, it remains one of my favorites along with two of Mother's best-known books, *The Good Earth*, and *The Living Reed*, the history of my people, Korea. *Fighting Angel* and *The Exile* also gave me a better understanding of Mother's parents, Absalom and Carie Sydenstricker. I thought it was sad that Mother's parents lived together for forty years and had seven children and yet lived such separate lives.

Mother also told me how she loved writing, not for writing's sake, but because she had a story to tell – a story, an idea, a feeling – that needed to be expressed on paper. Life in China struck Mother hard and deep, and she could freely write of those experiences in story form. Mother told me, "When I was a young girl, I enjoyed writing poetry more than prose." She also wondered what kind of poetry or prose she would have written if she had grown up in her grandparents' mansion in

West Virginia instead of living as the outcast daughter of American missionaries in China.

Mother felt her writing style reflected both her Eastern and Western upbringing. I pondered the fact, "I am from the East and from the West, just like Mother." This conversation ended by Mother asking to see my sketchbook. She was impressed with some of my work, and smiled as she looked at the sketch of her leg that I had just completed while listening to her reflect upon her childhood. That afternoon has remained a precious memory of my time with her. I still treasure the sketch of her leg resting on her ottoman.

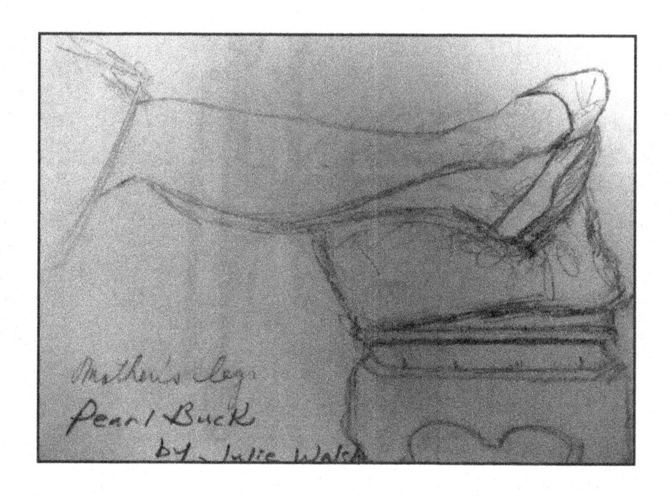

Julie's sketch of Mother Pearl's legs

Chapter Fourteen

Carol

The next day, when we were eating lunch together, Mother told me she was sorry for not being the kind of mother that I needed. Now in her late 70's, she said that she was more like my grandmother. I knew what she was trying to say, but she was the only stability I had in my life, and I loved her and clung to her.

I was still grieving the death of my Umma and Mother Pearl was now my second mother. She knew I loved her. Sometimes she would say, "I love you, Julie.... You are such a comfort to me."

Mother then said that she would be going to Vineland, New Jersey, tomorrow to visit Carol. Carol was Mother's only biological daughter. She told me it was about a two-hour ride to Vineland, to a school that was designed to help educate people with developmental disabilities, helping Carol to live as independently as she could. I could see Carol's resemblance to Mother in the picture she showed me in her bedroom. I liked her smile. Mother told me that Carol was born with PKU syndrome, which resulted in her slow mental growth and constant deterioration since Carol's PKU was not treated immediately at birth. At that time, doctors were unaware of PKU conditions.

Mother felt she had received very little help from her first husband and from the doctors she sought out. She felt desperate and hopeless. She just did not know how to help her daughter. Mother said, "When Carol was nine years old, I enrolled her at the Vineland Training School." Mother told me that later she wrote a book entitled *The Child Who Never Grew*. This book included her feelings as the mother of a child with special needs through all the experiences she had had with Carol. Mother told me she had been very concerned about paying for Carol's institutionalization and tuition. So, she started writing her first book, *East Wind, West Wind*. She said that many publishers were not interested in that type of writing. But Richard Walsh, who was the president of the John Day Publishing Company published *East Wind, West Wind*, and her next book as well, *The Good Earth*. More than 4,000,000 copies of that book were sold. *The Good Earth* became the window to China for several generations of Americans. This classic book earned Mother the Pulitzer Prize in 1932 and the Nobel Prize in Literature for all her published works in 1938. How proud I was of Mother when she told me that she was the first American woman to receive both the Pulitzer and Nobel prizes!

I asked mother why she wrote with the name Pearl S. Buck instead of her then married name, Pearl S. Walsh. She explained it this way. "I was married to John Lossing Buck for 18 years. He was an American agricultural missionary. He was a kind, but somewhat distant man and we went separate ways. Then, I married Richard Walsh." Richard Walsh's picture was in Mother's room with a pipe in his mouth. He looked like an insightful and kind gentleman. His intellect, resourcefulness, business sense, and support for Mother provided a very different life than she had been used to. Married to a publisher, she could become lost in her writing as they began to raise a large and international family.

My original question about Mother's use of her first husband's name resulted in her asking me what my middle name was. I had no idea what a middle name was. She told me that her middle name was Comfort, and her last name was Sydenstricker – her maiden name. And, that's why the "S." is between "Pearl" and "Buck."

Then Mother said that I needed a middle name and she said, "From now on, I'll call you Julie Comfort Walsh because you are such a comfort to me." I immediately liked the sound of that name. Mother had said that her full maiden name was Pearl Comfort Sydenstricker. Carol's middle name was also Comfort. At the time, I was a little confused, but at least I had a middle name – and I liked being a Comfort to my second mother.

I could understand the struggles Mother had helping Carol to get the best care she could for her only biological daughter. Was a cure to be found? Was something missing in the constant care Vineland offered? She had great tenderness towards Carol, who was now in a woman's body but had a childlike mind. Mother was quiet. Being apart from her daughter, saying good-bye to Carol at the end of their visits had to be so difficult. An institution like the Vineland Training Center was all that was available at the time to care for a young woman with a birth disability that offered little hope for any kind of independent life. I sensed these thoughts and struggles troubled Mother.

I quietly pondered too. Would Mother have written so many books if she were not concerned about the cost of Carol's tuition? Was Carol, whom Mother loved so deeply, a blessing to Mother and to us in that she wrote so many books largely due her and so we could enjoy her work? Without Carol, would Mother have ever begun writing *East Wind, West Wind?* Would she have ever written a book at all? Would there have been a "Pearl S. Buck?" Would there have been foundations bearing her name in six different Asian countries to help many Amerasians like me?

Mother often said, "I want all Amerasians to be educated so they could be productive citizens in their birth countries!" Without Carol, would I be in America, next to Mother in this comfy, beautiful home where I was being loved and cared for? Did Carol indirectly give me a second chance at life through my new mother? Thank you, Carol!

The next morning, Mother seemed a bit tired at breakfast. Was yesterday's trip to the Vineland Training Center too much for her? I wondered if she did not sleep too well. I asked, "Mother, are you OK?" She said that she was tired and would take a nap later in the afternoon. I remember thinking that there was a mix of mental, emotional, and physical tiredness in Mother's demeanor after her trip to Vineland.

At dinner that evening, I asked Mother if I could go to church on Sunday with a friend named Jeff. In giving me permission, she asked what church he and his family attended. When I told her, she proceeded to inform me that she had read through the entire Bible and was encouraged by her mother to memorize many Bible verses.

Mother felt Jesus was a wonderful humanitarian who truly gave women more honor and dignity than other leaders. Mother also felt sympathetic towards China. She did not agree or understand why American missionaries were bent on "saving" China.

At the church, I didn't understand what Jeff's pastor was talking about or the songs we sang but I did enjoy getting dressed up in a pretty dress. I often would pick a camellia to match my dress and decorate my hair with the beautiful fresh flower. At church, I would also go to Jeff's youth group, where we played different games. The kids were always friendly to me and it was good to be with them.

I signed up to try out for the girls' basketball team at my Pennridge High School. At our house, we had a basketball hoop set up in the barn, where I practiced and practiced! I was not very good. One cold day, we were practicing a drill in the gym where each girl would bounce the ball off the backboard. The next girl would jump, catch it, and put it back up off the backboard for the next girl. In my first turn, the ball came down at an angle. When I tried to catch it, I broke my left little finger! My pinky was at ninety degrees to my ring finger. That broken finger was the end of my practice, the end of my season, and the end of my short-lived basketball career.

I also enjoyed playing tennis. When I played alone, I used the wall upstairs in our big red barn, taking turns hitting and following through with my forehand and backhand. I also invited friends over to play tennis on our tennis court. In my 10th grade year, at Pennridge, I made the high school tennis team. It was good to be part of a team.

Julie on Pennridge Tennis Team
front row right with headscarf

Chapter Fifteen

Palmer House & The Prices

One day I had a meeting with our school's career guidance counselor and, when I came home from school, Mother and I began to talk about what kind of an educational future I might have. I told Mother that I would really like to major in math education in college. "Mother, I like kids and I enjoy solving math problems." Her answer, "Julie, it's important to know what you like best to do and find a way to make a living by it." I had shared the same interest in math with the guidance counselor earlier that day but had been told that I did not have enough math courses to be in a college bound academic track. I would have to go to summer school for two more courses, Algebra 1 and Algebra 2, before starting my senior year at Pennridge. Then, I would be prepared to enter the college of my choice.

Mother asked me to give her a little time to consider what options might be available. A few days later, mother told me about a boarding school in North Conway, New Hampshire that had a "summer school" at Wells Beach in Maine. There, with the other boarding school students, I could get the help I needed in extra math courses and also with my English skills before returning to Pennridge for my senior year. It sounded promising but I was not sure that I wanted to go and leave Mother and Green Hills Farm.

Unfortunately, my friendship with Jeff had become very difficult due to his involvement with drugs. I tried to help him but to no avail. Mother also heard that his drug use had become known to the local police department. She said to me, "While I hope it is not true, I ask you to be very careful to find out the truth. Maybe it would be a good thing for you to go away for a while." I thought perhaps all of this was happening to help me make my decision to go to Wells Beach and summer school.

Before leaving for summer school, Mother gave me her own suitcase inscribed with her initials, PSB. She also handed me a Korean scroll given to her by the Korean people. Mother wanted me to decorate my room with it. She also gave me her beautiful pearl pin. This is the pin she often liked to wear so elegantly in her hair. When Mother's beautiful, silvery hair was down, I couldn't believe how long it was! Now, she wanted me to have that pearl pin. What a treasure! I felt very sad to say good-bye to Mother, but I reminded myself that this would only be for the summer.

Pearl's suitcase, pearl hairpin and embroidered scroll.

Gifted to Julie upon entering The Palmer School, they are now on display at the Pearl S. Buck Memorial Hall in South Korea

The Palmer House Boarding School's summer school buildings were right by the ocean. As soon as I walked down seven steps, I was on the sand! Although much time was devoted to study, there was plenty of time for fun and activities. Collecting sea glass became a pastime of mine. The colors ranged from white, green, blue, pink, and anything between. To have its smooth shape, there must been so many years of "to and fro" with the incoming and outgoing tide. I also found myself enjoying sketching and water coloring, especially the lighthouses by the rocky cliffs of the Maine shore line. Something powerful, protective, and peaceful always drew me to the charm of the lighthouse.

The Palmer House School

The policy of the school was well-defined and strict. Somehow, I found myself not resenting it. The young men and young ladies were kept apart and we weren't allowed to date. I felt safe and secure in that environment.

Spending my summer running, sketching, and finding sea glass under the bright sun had tanned my skin much darker than I would like. My teeth and palms of my hands looked much lighter against my suntanned skin. I was conscious of not looking too Korean. While I lived in Korea, everyone only saw my American qualities, and I was ridiculed for being a "half-breed." Now, in America, I wanted to look more like an American and less Asian. Darker skin did not help me in that quest.

Summer was drawing to a close and it was time for me to return to Green Hills Farm in Pennsylvania for my senior year of high school. Mother and I had been corresponding a lot during the summer. For her health needs, she was spending much of time in her Vermont mountain home. Since Mother was rarely at home in Pennsylvania, I really had no desire to return there. I did not particularly welcome the thought of being in Perkasie, Pennsylvania, while Mother was 400 miles away in Vermont. The rules, the solitude, and the tranquility that I had felt and enjoyed at the boarding school made me want to stay at the Palmer House

School North Conway, New Hampshire site for the Fall semester. The insecurities I was feeling – especially with Mother's declining health – were bolstered by the secure four walls of my room and school. The strict, stable environment somehow gave me safety in my heart. I wrote to Mother requesting her permission to finish my senior year at the Palmer House School. Graciously, she granted my desire in a letter that she wrote to me. I missed Mother. I missed our conversations in her room, our special times having lunch, just the two of us. I missed playing games of chess and looking forward to the stamps she gathered for me. Mother comforted me by letting me know she would visit me as often as she could.

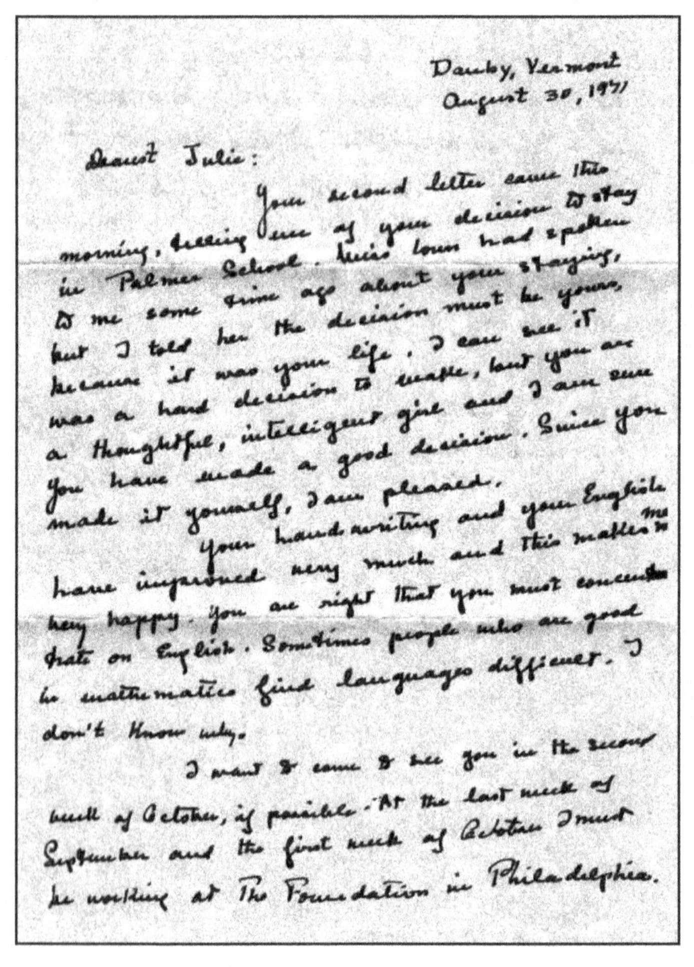

Danby, Vermont
August 30, 1971

Dearest Julie:

Your second letter came this morning, telling me of your decision to stay in Palmer School. Luis Lowe had spoken to me some time ago about your staying, but I told her the decision must be yours, because it was your life. I can see it was a hard decision to make, but you are a thoughtful, intelligent girl and I am sure you have made a good decision. Since you made it yourself, I am pleased.

Your handwriting and your English have improved very much and this makes me very happy. You are right that you must concentrate on English. Sometimes people who are good in mathematics find languages difficult. I don't know why.

I want to come to see you in the second week of October, if possible. At the last week of September and the first week of October I must be working at The Foundation in Philadelphia.

Autographed handwritten two-sided letter to Julie at the Palmer School from Pearl in Danby, Vermont, dated 8-30-71

Then I will return here in time to see
the beautiful autumn leaves, and that will
be a good time to come and see you, too.

Jean says she had a nice letter from
you and she appreciates this very much. I
Everyone there has been busy freezing vegetables for the winter.

The weather here is very cool and clear
and maybe summer is over. I am working
on a book as usual, and am busy. I
enjoy the cool air of Vermont and have
no hay fever here.

Dear Julie, I know you will do
your best.

With love,

Mother

Dearest Julie,

Your second letter came this morning, telling me of your decision to stay in Palmer School. Miss Loun had spoken to me some time ago about your staying, but I told her the decision must be yours, because it is your life. I see it was a hard decision to make, but you are a thoughul, intelligent girl and I am sure you have made a good decision. Since you made it yourself, I am pleased.

Your handwriting and your English have improved very much and this makes me very happy. You are right that you must concentrate on English. Sometimes people who are good in mathematics find languages difficult. I don't know why.

I want to come to see you in the second week of October, if possible. At the last week of September and the first week of October I must be working at The Foundation in Philadelphia.

Then I will return here in time to see the beautiful autumn leaves, and that will be a good time to come and see you, too.

Jean says she had a nice letter from you and she appreciates this very much. Everyone there has been freezing vegetables for the winter.

The weather here is very cool and clear and maybe summer is over. I am working on a book as usual, and am busy. I enjoy the cool air of Vermont and have no hay fever here.

Dear Julie, I know you will do your best.

With Love, Mother

September came, and I was in my new school by Crystal Lake in North Conway. Quickly I fell in love with the exquisite scenery. I spent much of my free time walking alone, sitting by the lake, reading and writing. The stillness of the lake and being alone with nature brought me immeasurable peace and joy. However, I often pondered, "Why am I here? What is my purpose in life?" The Palmer House School provided many cultural experiences for all thirty-two students from elementary to senior high school. I was the oldest and the only senior at the school.

Our weekends were often exciting, stimulating, and educational for us. From the Boston Symphony Orchestra, to the ballet, to cultural and historical museums, to nature hikes or just simply having a country night at school singing with the banjo and square dancing – we seemingly did it all! I also took ballet lessons twice a week. There, I made great efforts to discipline my body. Ballet required much tenacity and persistent work and I needed to learn to respond harmoniously to my body. I also learned to work in the photography darkroom. I learned how to take my photographs to their full development. This also took much time, precision, skill, and patience.

Our physical education requirement for the winter season was to ski. Every Thursday afternoon, from noon until five o'clock, we would ski at Wild Cat Mountain, right across from Mount Washington. I certainly was not "born to ski!" Why did the ski blades need to be so long? They were taller than me. But I progressed slowly to standing up on my skis and started to build up some confidence. Then, two of my friends collided right in front of me. Both broke their legs. I felt so bad for them and I was scared. Somehow, I found myself wanting to get sick on Thursdays!

After chapel services on Sunday, we were all free to do as we pleased. I spent most of my Sunday afternoons writing letters to Mother in Vermont, and to friends back home in Pennsylvania. One couple that received letters from me regularly were Mr. and Mrs. Price. I had met them when I visited the First Baptist Church in Perkasie, Pennsylvania. They were the sponsors of the youth group. My girlfriend from Pennridge attended this church and she invited me to her youth group's international dinner. I made Korean tempura that night. Mr. and Mrs. Price were very friendly and showed a genuine interest in me.

The Prices asked Mother if they could invite me to their house. Mother agreed, and they were able to take me out to a nice restaurant and then brought me back to my Green Hills Farm home. To thank them, I gave them a little tour of our house and then I took them to the green house and cut some flowers for them.

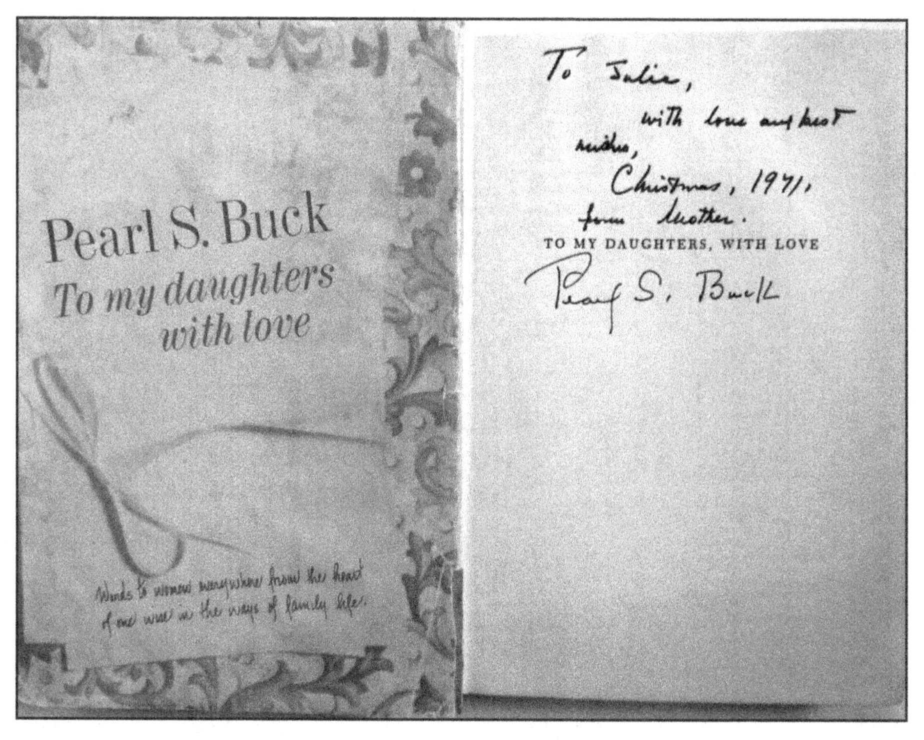

Precious gift of a signed copy, inscribed to Julie from Mother Pearl, of Pearl's book dedicated to all her daughters, dated Christmas, 1971.

During my senior year, one of the highlights was when the Prices would drive for eight hours to come up to visit me in New Hampshire. They were so glad to see me and I liked them very much! I later learned that the Prices and Mother had been talking a lot about me.

My senior year went by quickly and it was soon time to graduate. Since I was to be the only 1972 graduate, I was the best in the class and the worst in the class - I was also the most likely to succeed and the least likely to succeed! There was a beautiful banquet planned to honor the lone graduate, and the younger children had practiced so much to provide a delightful program for me. I even sang a solo, "*Tis a Gift to Be Simple.*" However, Mother was not feeling well and could not come. Mr. and Mrs.

Price did come along with their friend, Diane, and a friend I had met at Wells Beach the previous summer. I was so glad they were there to celebrate this very important event in my life. I was now the high school graduate that my Umma wanted me to be!

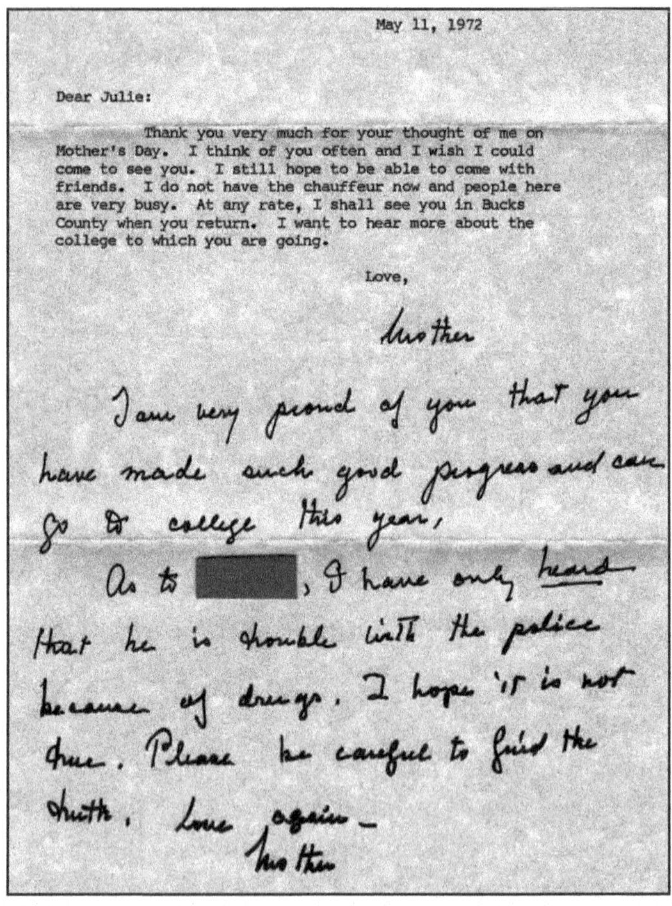

May 11, 1972

Dear Julie:

Thank you very much for your thought of me on Mother's Day. I think of you often and I wish I could come to see you. I still hope to be able to come with friends. I do not have the chauffeur now and people here are very busy. At any rate, I shall see you in Bucks County when you return. I want to hear more about the college to which you are going.

Love,

Mother

I am very proud of you that you have made such good progress and can go to college this year,

As to ______, I have only <u>heard</u> that he is trouble with the police because of drugs. I hope it is not true. Please be careful to find the truth. Love again –

Mother

Dear Julie: *May 11, 1972*

Thank you very much for your thought of me on Mother's Day. I think of you often and I wish I could come to see you. I still hope to be able to come with friends. I do not have the chauffeur now and people here are very busy. At any rate I shall see you in Bucks County when you return. I want to hear more about the college to which you are going. Love, Mother

I am very proud of you that you have made such good progress and can go to college this year.

As to ______, I have only <u>heard</u> that he is trouble with the police because of drugs. I hope it is not true, Please be careful to find the truth.
Love again - Mother

March 22, 1972

Miss Julie Walsh
Palmer House School
Conway, New Hampshire

Dear Julie:

Thank you very much for your letter. I am so glad Miss Loun came to see you, and as you know, I will certainly come to your graduation if I am in the country. We have not heard yet from China.

Yes, I have read OF HUMAN BONDAGE more than once. It contains much of Somerset Maugham's own personal experience as a child and young man and perhaps that is one of the reasons why it is such a good novel.

I called Jean and she is sending you some more chopsticks, since the other ones she sent seem to be lost in the mail.

With love,

Mother

Dear Julie: *March 22, 1972*

Thank you very much for your letter. I am so glad Miss Loun came to see you, and as you know, I will certainly come to your graduation if I am in the country. We have not heard yet from China.

Yes, I have read Of Human Bondage *more than once. It contains much of Somerset Maugham's own personal experience as a child and young man and perhaps that is one of the reasons why it is such a good novel.*

I called Jean and she is sending you some more chopsticks, since the other ones she sent seem to be lost in the mail.

With Love,
Mother

I was told that, if I wanted to live with the Prices after graduation, I was permitted to do so. My other option was to return to Green Hills Farm, where I would be under the supervision of my guardian, since by now Mother was living in Danby, Vermont almost full-time. Green Hills Farm was the most beautiful place I had ever lived. I missed everyone and I even missed my bedroom. But without Mother, it just was not the same place for me. I decided to accept their offer to go and live with them. Mother was glad that I had come to that decision on my own, and I could see the delight on the faces of Mr. and Mrs. Price.

On June 22, 1972, I arrived in Telford, Pennsylvania, about eight miles from Green Hills Farm – to my new home with Harry and Jean Price. This was a different living experience for me. There was a man in this family! This man daily showed how much he loved his wife. They often said kind things to each other and I noticed that they never seemed to argue or fight. I intently observed how they treated the other as more important than themselves.

Regularly, Mr. and Mrs. Price went to church and I accompanied them. Not just on Sunday morning, either. They also went to church on Sunday and Wednesday nights as well. Though I was raised in Korea to be a Buddhist and was permitted but not encouraged to go to church by Mother, I felt there was something missing in my life. What if my good deeds did not outweigh my bad deeds, as I had been cautioned against in my Buddhist heritage? During that first summer living with the Prices, I reflected each week upon the messages I heard in their church. I listened carefully but could not seem to put things together. I had no peace about what I was hearing. I even thought that the Prices were good Christians because they were old! To an eighteen-year-old, anyone over thirty was old. Later I found out that the Prices were in their early fifties.

A month after moving in with the Prices, I met Doug Henning. I sensed that he had a very special relationship with the Jesus that I heard so much about at church. Doug had peace and purpose in his life, something that I knew I did not have but was searching to find.

Mr. Price was a long-time member of the Souderton Area School Board. In 1971, while Doug was a junior at Souderton High School, Mr. Price visited a class where the rock opera, "*Jesus Christ, Superstar*" was being discussed. Doug was in this class along with nineteen other students and two teachers. This was a pioneer attempt at a combined American Cultures/English class for college bound juniors.

Mr. Price was impressed with the exchange between the students over the theme of the book – that Jesus was a radical teacher who wanted to see the world change but ended up dying by crucifixion because his kind of change was not acceptable. At Mr. Price's home, the discussion shifted to whether Jesus was the Son of God or not and did he resurrect from the dead? The out-of-class discussions continued into a Bible study during the summer before Doug's senior year. Although I did not know him at the time, while I was taking summer math classes at Wells Beach, Maine, Doug was in my future father's living room discussing his faith in God with his classmates.

When I came to live at the Prices' home, Mr. and Mrs. Price invited the now graduated members of that discussion group to a dinner in their home before they all headed off to college. I asked Mr. and Mrs. Price if I could prepare Korean food for the group. About half of the original twenty members of the class planned on being there.

When the dinner began, all but one of the planned attendees had arrived. The chair next to me was empty. Almost an hour into the meal, while everyone was at least curious about, if not enjoying the Korean food, the last person to the dinner arrived and sat next to me – the only seat available around the dining room table. He had nice looking blonde hair and his face was tanned. It had been a very hot and muggy day, and I found out that this guy had been late because his summer job of working on an asphalt paving crew had run overtime that Friday evening. I ended up going to the kitchen seven times to re-fill his tall iced tea glass! I was amused with this person who could drink so much! When I asked him his name, he said, "Doug." I thought he said, "Duck." So, I said, "You mean Duck, quack, quack?" while flapping my arms as if they were duck wings. The entire table broke out in laughter. I was glad that he had worked late that day with 300-degree blacktop paving in 97-degree temperature. That way, I was able to sit next to Doug and wait on him.

At the end of the evening, Mr. Price invited the group to come to his church on Sunday to hear him speak. Our church's pastor was on vacation and Mr. Price was taking his place. On Sunday, Doug was the only one of the group to attend. I was delighted. I found him to be very handsome, decent, and nice. Our church's youth group was going to Ocean City, New Jersey the following Saturday and another friend prodded me to ask Doug to come along. I did not need much prodding. I said, "Would you like to come with us?" He said, "Sure." That was our first date! Mr. and Mrs. Price seemed to be happy that I was dating a Christian guy. They said that they had been praying that I would meet a

Christian friend. They always used the word "praying" a lot. Mother Pearl had often talked of "divine guidance," something she could not clearly see.

Toward the end of that summer, our church offered a week-long evening Youth Bible Studies. By that time, I was now seeing Doug a few times each week and we attended these studies together. On the last evening, a Friday, we were sitting around a bonfire, only five weeks after we had met. The group was confronted with this question: "If you were to die today, and God asked, 'Why should I let you into my heaven?' what would you say?" That question really hit me hard. I thought to myself, "God, I try to be a good person to others. I do remember the time I stole a sweet potato from someone's farm in Korea because I was so hungry but I figured God would understand that one."

When I got home, I started reading the Bible. I found in the book of Isaiah the words, "All of our righteousness is like filthy rags." My righteousness and all my good deeds just didn't measure up. I also read, "For all have sinned and come short of the glory of God." It said ALL. That meant me, too! And then the Bible said, "For God so loved the world that He gave His only begotten Son, that whoever believes in Him would not perish but have everlasting life." I found myself wondering why this God would love me so much that He would sacrifice His Son for me. As a Buddhist, I never felt I could be sure that I had a guarantee of paradise someday. But the Bible said that whoever *believed*, not whoever *worked hard*, would have eternal life.

At that moment, I wanted to believe. But, what if it's not true, and it's only a fairy tale? Then, I read from the Bible, that Jesus said, "I am the way, the truth, and the life. No man comes to the Father, but by me." He said He is THE Way, and no one else. I remember Mr. Price once told me, "What does it profit a man if he gains the whole world, but loses his soul?" I surely did not want to lose my soul! That very night, I said, "Oh, God. I do not understand everything. But I choose to believe that Jesus is your Son. And, He chose to die on the cross to pay the penalty for all my sins. Please forgive me and make me your child." Could there be a Savior for an unwanted Amerasian like me? Words were inadequate to express the gratitude I was feeling. I simply trusted Jesus to be my Savior.

Soon after, Doug left to attend Bloomsburg State College and I stayed in my new home and attended Montgomery County Community College, which was close by. Although, through Mother, I had been accepted at West Virginia Wesleyan College and Blackburn College in Illinois, it was the best decision for me to stay close to home with my new "family." I commuted in the morning with another local girl who became a good friend, and Mr. Price would pick me up in the afternoon. The ride was about thirty minutes and it was a good chance for us to talk and really get to know each other. The more I learned about the Prices, the more I discovered that they were kind people of principle and willing to help all people in need. They genuinely tried to live by what the Bible taught and I grew to love them dearly.

Chapter Sixteen

Pearl's Death & My Adoption

Mother died from lung cancer on March 6, 1973. I knew she had not been well and I knew that someday this day would come. But, when it came, I could not find words to describe the emotions I was feeling. If I could only have been with her when she was dying. I wish I could have been holding her hand. I have now lost two mothers. "Oh God! How much more can I take?"

Mother's death occurred almost nine months after I had come to live with the Prices. It was difficult enough struggling with Mother's death, but I also found out that I was not legally adopted. I had always thought since my name was Julie Walsh – Julie "Comfort" Walsh – after Mother's middle name, that I was an adopted daughter of Pearl S. Buck. My social security card even said, Julie Comfort Walsh. What about all the times she introduced me to others as, "My daughter." Apparently, in the early 1970's, Pennsylvania law did not allow a single woman to legally adopt. However, I did not learn that until after Mother's death. "No matter, Mother. That's only in name. I know what we had together. O-O-O-h, Mother!"

Mother's gravesite was on the grounds of Green Hills Farm. I needed to visit Mother's grave. I needed to tell her how much I missed her. I wanted to thank her for being my second mother after my Korean Umma had died and I had needed so badly for someone to love me. "Mother, do you remember the time when we first met? What about the time you came to pick me up at the airport and I couldn't even wear my shoes? How your eyes twinkled with your smile when you saw my swollen feet from the airplane ride. Your eyes, your beautiful blue eyes, got larger and larger when I needed your signature to go to the zoo.

I kept saying the 'ju' – you tried so hard to understand me but could not – until I finally said, 'animal house.' How we laughed!

Do you remember the time we searched everywhere to find your pearl hairpin only to find it in your bedroom's trash can? How often you had to come to my room and turn out the lights because I fell asleep while studying. Mother, one night I wasn't quite asleep and I saw how long and silky your silvery hair was when it hung down."

At a White House dinner on April 29, 1962, for American winners of the Nobel Prize, from left novelist Pearl S. Buck conversing with President John F. Kennedy, and first lady Jacqueline Kennedy exchanging greetings with poet Robert Frost before the after-dinner program. (The Associated Press)

"How I loved to hear you tell of your visit to the White House with President Kennedy. You felt that he did not quite understand the tensions between the Koreans and the Japanese. And, you let the President know about the lingering problems in the Far East!"

"I am sorry, Mother, that you did not get to go back to China. How you wanted to visit your beloved country once more. It saddens me still that you were unable to go. Your desire was to visit the land you spent so much of your life living as a missionary's daughter. I understand that. I long to see Korea again, too!"

"Mother, Mr. and Mrs. Price are so very good to me. Thank you for taking care of me even when you were not well. You arranged for me to be cared for by the Prices, because you weren't feeling well. Where would my life have been if you hadn't intervened when I was in Korea?

"Oh God, I thank you for my Mother Pearl, who made all the difference in my life. She brought me to America where I would not be scorned for being of mixed race. Most importantly, she loved me just as I was. Thank you, thank you, Mother…I love you! You will always live in my heart."

Oil portrait by Freeman Elliott of Pearl S. Buck that hangs over the mantlepiece today in the Cultural Center.

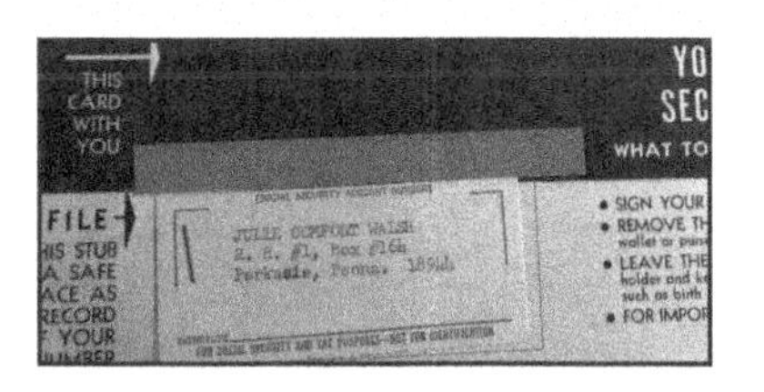

Julie's Social Security card

Julie Henning visiting Mother Pearl's graveside on the grounds of Green Hills Farm.

In the summer of 1973, I was adopted by the Prices – this time it was official with court-approved papers and all! They had never been able to have a child of their own. They told me that they had prayed that someday God would send them a child. This child came at the age of nineteen! In order to go through with my adoption, I found out that I still needed a birth certificate. After much consultation with a lawyer, he suggested that the easiest way for me to have a birth certificate was to create a new one that stated Mrs. Price – who had never been to Korea – gave birth to me in Pusan, Korea! It worked, and I now had a birth certificate that said I was born to Jean Price on May 14, 1954 in Pusan, Korea.

It was wonderful to have another mother, but now also someone I could also call my father, for the first time in my life. Though I felt somewhat uncomfortable, I found myself seeking and needing their approval. I was often insecure. I realized that the many years of rejection and ridicule, not being wanted by my mother's country and not having a father didn't go away overnight, just as it is not easy to straighten a bent tree. I called my new parents Umma and Oppa, the Korean names for Mom and Dad. "Thank you, God, for always providing me with someone to love and to care for me, and someone for me to love. How can I ask for more?"

Chapter Seventeen

Doug Henning & Our Wedding

Doug did not have a car during his freshman year at Bloomsburg. But he hitchhiked home every weekend that he could, even when it took him 4-5 hours for what is usually no more than a two-hour drive. It was the beginning of our friendship and I so longed to be with him on the weekends that he could come home. We purchased two copies of the same Bible study guide and we studied together, discussed together, and prayed together. It was interesting to learn about the Bible, but the studying together also helped us to learn about each other in a more meaningful way. And my love for Doug grew stronger each day.

While I was also completing all the prerequisites courses that I needed in order to transfer to a four-year college, I also was learning much about God through reading the Bible. The Bible to me was like a love letter from God directly to me. As the sunflower seeks after the sun, so I desired to know the things the Bible had to say.

It was not so much that I wanted to be a Bible scholar – although it would be a worthy goal – I just wanted to spend time with the God who loves me so much and redeemed me and adopted me as His child. I felt as though God created a vacuum in my heart that only He could fill. He alone could give me peace in my insecure heart. I did not understand everything, but I was very enthusiastic about what I was learning and wanted to share what God was doing for me and to tell others that He loves us all.

I used to get into much discussion with my philosophy professor at the community college. As I look back, I may have sounded uninformed to him, but I wanted to share my new found hope that we can have in God. The philosophy professor at my graduation told my parents that I "almost" converted him to be a Christian. I am sure it was supposed to be a kind statement, but I was sad that "almost" was not "enough."

My desire for knowing God and studying the Bible became deeper. After looking into many different Christian Colleges, I chose to attend The King's College in Briarcliff Manor, New York.

Diane Bishop was six years older than me. She was a nurse who had boarded with my parents for five years before I had come to live with them, this was the same Diane who had accompanied my parents to my Palmer House School graduation. Diane and I became very close. Now, God even blessed me with a sister that I had never had before! In two years, I had learned to love my new parents and sister, however, now leaving them to go away to college was another new separation that I faced with uncertainty. It is hard for me to ever get used to leaving the ones I love. I never want to get used to that.

Jimmy Dirotto was one of the conference speakers we had at The King's College chapel. He was a very dynamic speaker and God used him to really speak to my heart, to give all my heart to God, and not just part of it. How often did I obey God just partially? I asked God to help me live my life the way He wanted me to live. I wanted my life to reflect God's love. Soon, my college life became very full. Besides my credit load studies, I became actively involved in sharing what the Bible said about God to senior citizens in their communities, visiting different colleges to share God's word, being involved in on-campus Bible studies at The King's, and always my own regular Bible study and prayer time.

One day I got a notice in my mailbox that I was nominated for Homecoming Queen. I couldn't believe what I read. I felt very honored but told myself not to get too excited. I am the one who, for most of my life, was teased and not wanted because of how I looked. I often felt very insecure about my appearance, but I felt it was a God-given opportunity to run for Homecoming queen and I decided to accept the nomination.

The next challenge was to come up with something for the talent show. Too long I had struggled just to survive the poverty of Korea and then to move to America and learn English, that I really didn't have any "talent" to speak of. After praying for God's guidance, the only thing I felt that I could do as a talent and that would be something unique to my college classmates would be Korean Folk Dance.

As a little girl, I loved to perform in front of my mother. She seemed happy to see me dance around the little room. I had watched people doing Korean folk dances, while I was still in Korea. So, I borrowed a Korean audio tape and choreographed a folkdance. I still had my Korean dress – a Hanbok – that had been given to me by my beloved Korean math teacher as a parting gift when I left for America six years earlier. She was so good to me!

Doug escorting Julie as the Junior Homecoming Queen at The King's College Homecoming

Vintage roadster used to transport the Homecoming Court at The King's College Homecoming

Now, with a brightly colored costume, Asian Music, and an unusual dance, I received enough votes to represent the Junior class for the Homecoming event. Doug was able to get away from Bloomsburg for the weekend and escorted me. We enjoyed riding around in the parade in an antique car. "Thank you, Lord, for helping me to be accepted by my peers." The King's College in Briarcliff Manor, New York and Bloomsburg, Pennsylvania were about 4 hours apart, but the distance between us did not stop our love from growing. In days, LONG before texting and internet, we called each other from dorm room phones and wrote letters almost every day. My Doug was a most patient, considerate and loving man.

My love for Doug grew stronger every day. One year after graduation from each of our colleges, we were married. June 25, 1977 was one of the happiest days of my life! Most brides-to-be would have many ideas about what kind of wedding dress they would desire, but I was too naïve about such matters. Some of my girlfriends would talk about what kind of wedding they dreamt of or what pattern for plates of silverware they desired. Somehow, I didn't seem to know what I wanted. I was not accustomed to choosing things for myself. So, Doug and I asked my parents for some help.

We had a memorable wedding! More than 300 people came and although I did not know most of them, I so appreciated that they were there. We hope they appreciated it equally. It was a June Saturday, with 95 degrees and 95% humidity, and the 300 guests were crammed into wooden pews in a non-airconditioned church!

Doug and I felt we were the host and hostess, so we did not set up a separate table for the bridal party. We wanted to serve our guests. So, we went around with a tray of goodies for people to enjoy. I could have never imagined how fast a day could go by. When we arrived at a hotel for a night before heading for our honeymoon destination, we were exhausted. My face even hurt from all the smiling!

But one of the things that I will always cherish is the fact that after my husband carried me over the door, we knelt together and prayed for God's guidance and blessing for our marriage and that our lives together would be a blessing to others.

God heard our prayers and He has truly blessed our marriage. There have been many difficult events and struggles in our lives, and through the struggles of my insecurities, God has blessed me with a wonderful, loving, steady husband. He is truly a blessing and the love of my life. He is a terrific father to our two wonderful sons, two lovely daughters-in-our-hearts, an awesome Pop-Pop to our five terrific grandsons, and loyal and loving to his brothers, sisters, nieces, and nephews.

I am so very thankful how my husband honors God with his life. He has such a strong faith and a gentle, true heart. I love the way that he prays for others, helps others, and encourages others. He shows so much grace and wisdom as he gives them counsel. I love and respect the compassionate pastor that he is. I find myself each day being thankful to God for the love God has given us to share. Throughout our marriage, I find myself loving who I am when I am with my husband.

Mr. and Mrs. Douglas Henning coming down the aisle.

Julie and Douglas Henning

The Henning Family
back row, L to R: Lydia, Jim, Chick, John
front row L to R: Helen, Julie, Doug & Paul (Chick)

Chapter Eighteen

Douglas, David, Daniel & Peter

For our first two years of marriage, we had a cozy apartment in the attic of a girlfriend's house. Six months into our marriage, she was expecting her baby at any time. While we were sleeping on a late Sunday evening, we were awakened by her screaming. My husband asked me to go downstairs to see if I could be of help. Our landlord and his wife were having their baby.

The baby came so fast, she didn't even have time to go to the hospital. Her husband called for the ambulance and for her friend who was a nurse. For the first time in my life, I helped to deliver a baby. The ambulance attendants came and took the mother and baby girl to the hospital. It was an absolute miracle to see a new life being born. I was so excited that I could hardly sleep. I kept saying to my husband, "I wish I were pregnant." Two weeks later, I found out that I already was! We were so thankful to God that we were going to have a baby, our baby.

But I soon got sick – sicker than I had ever been in my life. I had almost unbearable nausea that got worse as the day progressed. No matter what my doctor prescribed, it did not help. In my second month of pregnancy, I was unable to retain water. My doctor admitted me to the hospital for intravenous feeding since I was becoming dehydrated. I remember how long it took for the nurse to find my vein. It had shrunk so much. Trying to bear nausea and weakness was one thing, but trying to cope with the fear that something might be wrong with our baby gave us many sleepless nights. I found myself continuously praying to the Lord for the health of our baby.

By the third month of my pregnancy, I had lost twenty pounds. I began to wonder where my baby was getting his/her nourishment?

My condition was described as hyperemesis gravidarum. I struggled with persistent nausea and vomiting that wouldn't stop for the entire nine months, but I knew there would be an end to this. I developed a sympathy during that time for people who have chronic illnesses. As much as I wanted my daily living to be spiritually filled and to be a godly woman, I found that so often, my physical discomfort took over any desire I might have to be God's best.

The due date for our baby came but there was no sign of an appearance of a son or daughter yet! Two more weeks went by and the baby had not yet even dropped! My doctor ordered an x-ray which showed that my Asian pelvic bone was too narrow to have the baby's head pass through. I was disappointed that I could not have a natural child birth, but thankful that I could safely deliver via caesarian section.

Doug and I had faithfully attended classes and diligently practiced breathing exercises for a natural birth, but that wasn't what God had planned for us. After praying much, God gave me a peaceful heart to face the fear I had of the surgery, and eventually a thankful heart that the doctors had the wisdom to take care of us. I could understand the stories of mothers who died along with their child at birth.

I was thankful to God for another chance at life for my baby and me. Our son, Douglas Paul Henning, was born on October 4, 1978. He weighed 8 lbs. 10 oz. and was 22 inches long. He was such a beautiful child, and my husband and I were so elated to receive God's precious gift He had entrusted to us. How thankful we were! The birth of a baby is one of God's greatest miracles.

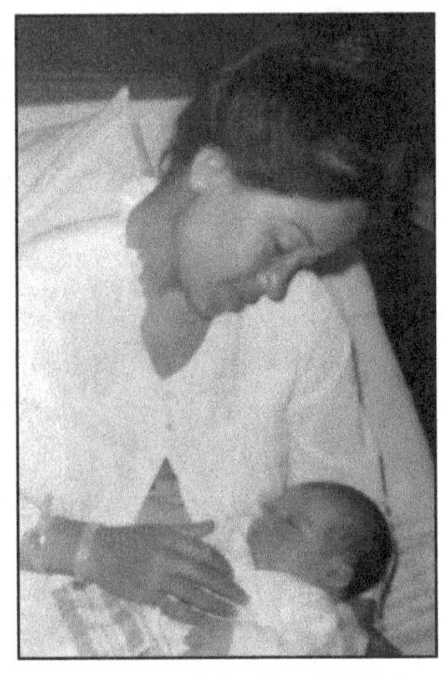

Julie and Douglas Paul Henning

Just prior to Douglas's birth, I had stopped working at the bank. My husband and I strongly felt that I should stay at home to give stability to our home and family. How wonderful that Douglas had a father who loves him dearly and even grandparents, uncles, aunts. Being with Douglas was such a precious time for me. But, for me to stay home was a blow to our financial picture! My husband's third year teaching salary gave us just enough to live on but being able to save money for a down payment for a house seemed far away. Living in an attic as a couple was easy, but, with a baby, it became more difficult as our son got bigger.

I began to sell Avon door-to-door pushing Douglas in his stroller until he got too curious and wanted to touch everything in customers' houses. Then I started working as a waitress three nights a week at a brand new, locally-owned restaurant, while my husband took care of our baby. When Douglas was eight months old, we purchased a small, old house. Despite its condition, it was home for us. We made it warm and loving. This is what I had prayed for since I was a little child – before I even knew the God I now love. I have a husband, a child, a family, and a home. God answered my prayers. How wonderful and gracious He is! We had a cozy home filled with love. For the first time in my life, I felt that it was all mine. I found myself wanting to hold onto it so tightly. But God was graciously teaching me that all things belong to Him, and that I was to be a good steward of what He had entrusted to me. "Oh, God. Thank you for blessing me with this loving family and home."

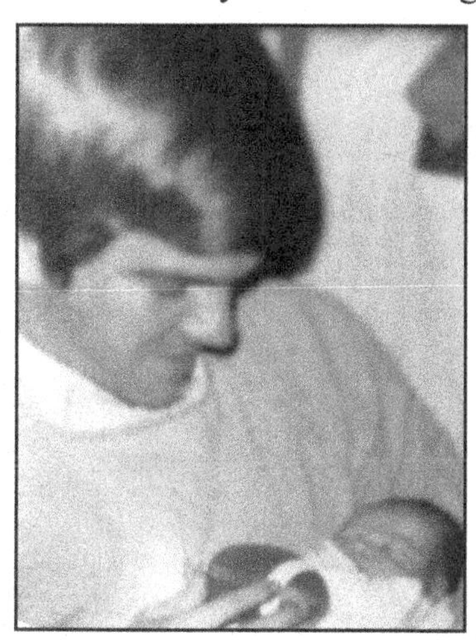

Doug and Douglas

God's blessings didn't stop there. God gave me a great number of relatives on both sides of our family. Not only was Douglas the first grandson for both our parents, but he also had many aunts and uncles who loved him and spoiled him to death! "God, you are so good to me. How thankful I am for your love and provisions in my life." As I was growing up, the only blood relative I had was my Umma and no one else. My mom and I were together, alone against the society in which we were placed. Now, I can even attend family gatherings and reunions. How precious those times are for me!

God also gave me another family, a precious group of believers in our local church – the church where we were married. There, we worshipped God together, learned of His Fatherly love and protection, and experienced the family fellowship of one-another's love, kindness, warmth, friendliness, and genuine care.

But even though I had all this love and acceptance of people around me, I still felt insecure. Sometimes, when I would say hello to people, for some unknown reason if they didn't reply, I would think, "What's wrong with me?" I was hard on myself and would get into a deep feeling of sadness. Each time, my husband would listen and talk to me calmly, assuring me that I should not be so sensitive – others have their own issues and that may be why they don't respond to me.

Somehow, though, I could not change my emotions overnight. We would talk about this over and over. We both felt that the reason I felt so insecure was perhaps all the rejections that I experienced as a child and that I was now going through a desperate need of acceptance. Thankfully, my husband offered me his full love and acceptance. His quiet, sensitive, consistent loving way showed me that I was accepted and loved dearly by God and him.

Then a few strange incidences happened to me. Late at night, as I would be talking to Doug, some of the uncomfortable childhood memories came back to me as if I were re-running a video. How often I broke down in tears. I didn't want to remember those awful memories. Somehow, they had been pushed way back in my memory bank. Now, feeling more secure, they were coming back. Somehow, I felt burdens being lifted from my heart. Somehow, I was beginning to understand myself, my thoughts, my actions and my behaviors.

One night, Douglas was asleep in his crib and I went into the nursery to make sure he was alright. Looking at him, I could almost see my Korean Umma's face in Douglas. My eyes flooded with tears. "Oh, Umma, how I miss you! Oh, how I wish you could see your grandson. He is such a good baby, so adorable. Oh, how I love him so. My husband loves me very much also, Umma. How proud you would be of your grandson and your son-in-law! We are family, Umma, and a very wholesome one at that, too. That is something that you could never have and you so wished it for me.

Oh, how I understand the love you had for me, so much more now, having a child of my own. The depth of your love for me was deeper than I knew. It is why you took your life to free me from you. You didn't want me to be in the same bondage you were in. Oh, how I wish you were here!"

"We have more good news, Umma. We are expecting twins! Can you believe it? Your daughter is going to have twins. Doug's parents were elated because they have twin sons, too. My adopted parents are glad also, but I can see the concerns in their eyes as they see how uncomfortable I am."

Doug, Douglas & Julie, already pregnant with twins

My parents' concerns became a reality. Three days after I had a good regular check-up, I started feeling such a tightness around my stomach that would not go away. I kept thinking it would stop hurting, but this severe a discomfort went on for days.

When I called my doctor, he told me to take some milk of magnesia. My husband rushed to the drugstore to get it. When he returned and I read the ingredients, I did not think it would do any good for me to take it. My doctor told me that I was of a small frame and would just have to bear up under the pain and discomfort. I was up for two full days without sleep and I could not find any position that would give me relief. My back felt as though someone was tearing my muscles.

My husband could not bear to see me in this agony any longer and took me to the Emergency Room of our local hospital where I got some pain shots. I am not the one to take medicine of any kind unless absolutely necessary but I found myself begging for more pain shots. Our babies' heart rates were checked every two to three hours. Forty-eight hours agonizing hours went by in the hospital maternity wing.

Finally, on Day 3, my doctor's associate came in to check on me. He thought we should have a c-section NOW. But, when we asked my primary OBGYN doctor, he hesitated to do anything yet since the babies were only seven and one-half months. He kept reiterating that the longer the babies are in my womb, the better. We did not know anything but to agree, and trusted God and the doctor to take good care of our twins.

He realized that I needed to have some amniotic fluid removed, but it was the day after Christmas, a Friday, and I'd need to wait till the full hospital staff came back the following Monday. But our babies could not wait two more days! Late Friday afternoon, December 26, 1980, our babies' heart rates got really fast and later on, one of the heartbeats was hard to find. Within a short time, my blood pressure doubled, and I was shaking so much that the nurses called the doctors. Finally, when my doctor arrived, five other physicians were checking on me. As I was wheeled into the surgery room, I thought that finally, they are going to take my twins before they are in any more danger. My doctor, I thought, came to the point where he realized that it is better to have them born at seven and one-half months than to continue with faster heartbeats in my womb.

When I woke up from surgery, my husband's moist eyes met mine and he said, "Honey, our boys did not make it." I just could not believe what my ears just heard. It just cannot be true. "No! No." I couldn't even cry. Our twin sons were stillborn.

I was given an opportunity to see my boys and hold them. So beautifully formed! How still they lay in my arms. "Oh God, why?" The doctors told us that they had never seen so much fluid in a womb before. They said that when they opened me up, the amniotic fluid gushed out like a fire hydrant. They collected the fluid from the operating room and found it to be four to five more times than normal. They suggested us to autopsy our twins to know what was wrong to try to prevent the same thing from happening in our next pregnancy.

Grave of our twin sons
David & Daniel

The autopsy came back with no cause of death from the health of the boys. Everything was normal. Then, what killed our twins? Somehow, they figured out that either I created way too much fluid, or the twins weren't using it efficiently. I was first placed back into maternity, but at my husband's request, the hospital staff allowed me to heal from my second c-section in an area of the hospital that was far enough away from the sound of crying babies. One of the hardest things my husband ever had to do was to bury our boys while I was still in the hospital.

I felt so numb, I could not even cry. Our identical twin boys, David and Daniel, were gone. Our boys were perfectly formed and weighed 4 lbs 11 oz and 5 lbs 2 oz. "Oh God, if only the c-section was performed on just the day before – on Christmas Day – while the heartbeats were still normal." We can see so much more clearly in hindsight!

Many family members and friends felt that it was my doctor's misjudgment. Some felt we should sue the doctor. But was that going to bring our twins back? Some say that the doctor needed to be taught a lesson, but what are you supposed to do with the money from a lawsuit? Shall we buy a new home from the death of our twins? We didn't want any money gained from our boys' deaths. We just wanted a doctor with an understanding heart.

However, my doctor didn't come to see me for two long days. Doug and I thought that perhaps he was having a hard time himself but we soon found out that did not seem to be the case. He never once said he was sorry or commented on the twins. Instead, he said, "Julie, you are young. You can have more children." Oh, I felt as though I could scream at him. How cold and thoughtless could he be? Yes, God could bless us with more children, but what about these precious souls who never had the opportunity to live outside the womb?

When parents lose a child of some age, they need to survive with the memories of the past. When parents lose children at birth, they need to deal with all the anticipation of what might have been. We lost the anticipation of life that David and Daniel were so ready to live. Although my doctor was so cold and insensitive to us, we felt that we should write him a letter, saying that we understand a human's frailty in judgment and that we did not hold him responsible, for it is God who controls and allows all things. We felt if part of God's plan for us was for our twins to live, they would have survived any of our doctor's misjudgments as well of a lack of holiday hospital staff.

I tried to accept the fact that the death of our twins was within God's permissive will, but how do I stop from missing them? And, how do I stop crying? How do I stop crying? How I wish I could just run and run away and never stop. I wished so hard to escape from the reality as though it had never happened. But there was our Douglas, our wonderful two-year-old son who needed me. I needed to be there for him. Oh, how precious he was! Without him, I think I could have gone mad.

And, I needed to give emotional support to my husband as he did for me. How often I thanked God for my husband and precious Douglas. What a good boy! Many people would often ask how I was doing, but what about my husband? Men hurt too, when they lose their children. We often wept together and cried ourselves to sleep. I thought I was accepting the reality and coping, but I found myself getting angry at God.

I kept on thinking for what purpose did God take our babies? If they were to die at birth, why was I allowed to carry them for more than thirty weeks with much physical difficulty? I had no babies to hold in my arms, but I still had to stop the milk from flowing and deal with the fatigue and discomfort of c-section incisions.

My pastor had explained that when a tea kettle boils, you need to let the steam out. If not, it will eventually burst. I needed to let out and express all that was turning and churning inside of me. I had to tell God that I felt angry, angry at Him for allowing this to happen in our lives. As I poured out all the thoughts, feelings, and emotions that were within me, somehow, I began to feel at peace. God understood my pain. He gave me His love, as I was reminded of the fact that He gave up his Son for me. Slowly, I felt that I could cope. God understood how I was hurting. "How could all these things work together for good, Oh, God?" For now, I just have to trust Him. May I be caring, sensitive and comforting to others who suffer.

While I became pregnant for a third time, I also became a naturalized citizen. On May 19, 1982, I became a citizen of the United States of America. At age 28, I finally became the citizen of a country! I could call America MY country. God bless America! Often, I hear about the ills of our nation, but I know of no land which is better, which gives me more freedom of choice and opportunity for me or anyone to become whatever I can with hard work.

Two months later, on July 9, God blessed us with a healthy baby! How many sleepless nights had I needlessly worried about the coming of this baby to full life? "Oh, thank you, God. Thank you for this precious bundle of life you have entrusted to us." Peter Brent Henning was born at 8 lbs, 21 inches long, so adorable and beautiful he was!

Peter was three and one-half years younger than Douglas. Douglas had dark hair, but Peter had the lightest of blonde hair with the sweetest smile, so content and happy I often said to him, "How is my "happy" doing today?"

How fascinated they were with each other. Peter followed whatever his older brother did, and Douglas was the best older brother anyone could have.

Doug, Julie, Douglas and Peter too, at Julie's naturalization ceremony on May 19, 1982

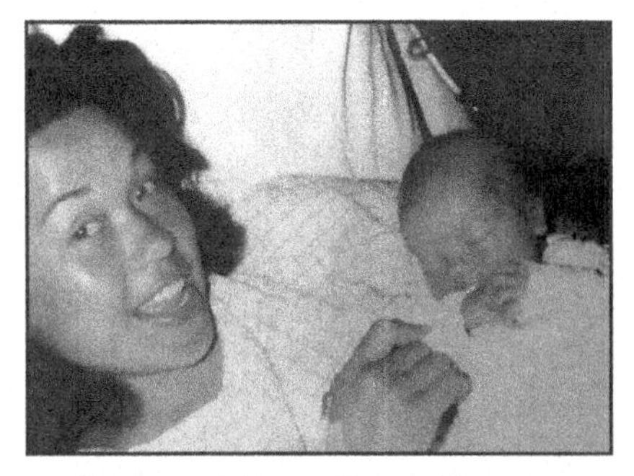

Julie and Peter Brent Henning

How often I wished we could have kept them both in a glass bottle and for time to just stand still.

What pride and joy they gave their parents! "Umma, we have the two most wonderful, adorable sons. They are such good boys! Oh, how I wish you could be here so you could love them and they could love you."

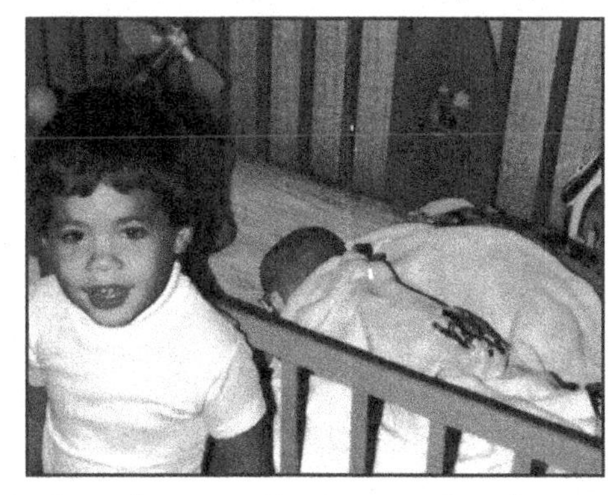

Douglas was always guarding Peter

Peter and Julie

Peter and Douglas

Henning Brothers
Through the Years

Pete and Doug

Doug and Pete

Chapter Nineteen

Congressional Hearing & Carnegie Hall

America is a place where you can fight for the rights that you feel you deserve. I was asked by the director of the Pearl S. Buck Foundation to testify before a Congressional hearing in Washington, D.C. The goal of this hearing was to give better status to Amerasians entering the United States. Doctors and scientists had preferential treatment over students and others. And, an Amerasian – who is half American and half Asian – is one-half, "red-blooded American." But Asian culture refers to them as American and American culture refers to them as Asian. Amerasians are at the bottom of the list in immigration status.

Most Amerasians did not even have a birth certificate as proof of their existence. I was praying to God for me to have the right words to speak before this hearing of U.S. Congressmen. Somehow, I needed these senators and representatives to realize the plight that Amerasians were facing in their mother countries. God did give me the words to speak. I was nervous and scared to speak to all these people in this awesome-looking building where what you say is recorded. The people listened, and I could see some sympathetic faces.

The next question that came up before the hearing was, "How can we tell who is Amerasian and who is not?" The men and women were talking about all different kinds of blood tests and the like. I realized that Congress needed to find a definite way to find out which of these "Asian-looking" immigrants truly had American parentage. I was getting frustrated because my own thinking was, "You just need to look at Amerasians to see the American portion of their faces."

The meeting went on and on, and I eventually realized that it was not such a simple matter. Solving this problem involved identifying exactly who was entitled to claim status as the child of an American and an Asian parent. The year that I came to America, 1968, there were so many Amerasians left in Korea. I am sure that there are more by now! "God, please help these children, grown men and women who have to face the injustices of life because of the color of their skin, their eyes, or their hair."

How often the unknown produces fear and fear produces prejudice. We have to find solutions to help Amerasians in this plight. I know adoption alone would not solve the problem. My own history is proof of that. I am so thankful that the Pearl S. Buck Foundation developed a program of child sponsors so that the Amerasian children can be educated in their own country with an opportunity to be productive, useful citizens of the land of their birth. Then, perhaps someday the prejudice would be lessened. Most of the time, mothers and children were so poor that putting a morsel of food in their mouths became the most important priority. Just like my Umma.

Somehow, I needed to let the American public know how many people with half-American blood are suffering in Asian countries. I have learned over the years that American people are generally compassionate people who would give of their time and resources to help the needy and would fight for causes that led to justice for the targeted or oppressed around the world, including the Amerasians. Or would they?

These Amerasian children are the children of their sons and husbands! If I were the wife of a soldier in the 1980's who had fathered a child in Korea during the Korean War thirty years earlier, how would I respond? As sobering as that thought is to me, I must let the public know of the difficulty facing Amerasian children in Korea and other Southeast Asian countries, where Pearl S. Buck International now runs child sponsorship and support programs.

Again, God heard my prayers! Pearl Buck's Foundation was assumed under the umbrella of Pearl S. Buck International. I received a phone call from them asking me to appear on a WCAU radio program in Philadelphia to share my life as it was in Korea.

I was so grateful for the chance. Perhaps to let the American public know of the difficult life facing Amerasians was one of the reasons I was brought to the States. I had never been to a radio station before.

We passed through a noisy room full of people talking and typing away. Beyond the narrow hallway, we entered a small room and the door was completely shut. There was nothing in this room except a table, chairs, and a large clock on the wall. The interviewer, Susan Brey, asked me if I was nervous. I just nodded my head with a smile. Somehow, I knew that when the time came, God would give me the right words to say. At least, I hoped for that!

When we came onto the air, it felt awkward talking into a microphone. I pretended I was just talking to Susan. There was a question about my father's whereabouts. I tried to control my emotions, but I couldn't stop the tears from choking my throat at that question. I told her I didn't know where he was. I hoped in my heart that he was still alive in the early 1980's. I miss him so – someone I never knew! I just longed to see him once, even once. I would introduce myself to him. The hour on the air went fast! I prayed that the listeners would understand more about the discrimination that Amerasians face in their mother countries and the lack of hope they have for their futures, unless other people cared.

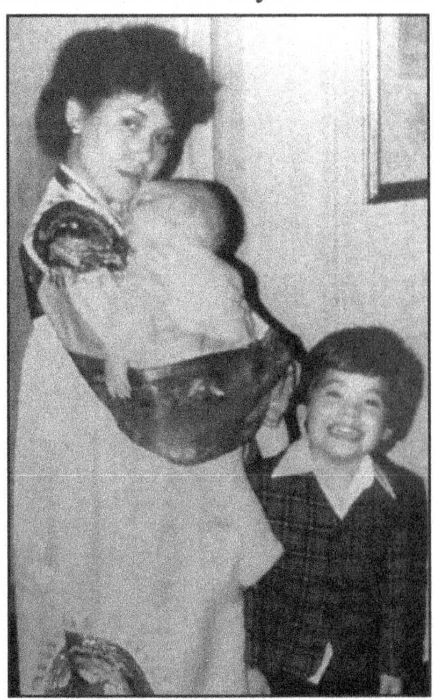

Julie, Peter and Douglas

Soon after that, another opportunity was offered to me. I was asked to speak at Carnegie Hall in New York City to more than 3,000 attendees in February of 1983. I wore my Korean dress and I carefully wrote out pages of notes of what I was going to say and tried to memorize it.

Since I knew my English was still not proficient, I wanted to speak properly. But, when I began to speak before all those people and seeing their faces, my rehearsed speech just stopped. At that time, I knew that I just had to say what was in my heart, even if my English wasn't always correct. I knew that I was speaking from my heart to their hearts and they listened. That night, I prayed and hoped that there would be a better understanding about the plight of Amerasians, and that people in

America would actively work to make our Amerasian lives better either here in America, or Korea. My husband, Douglas, and seven-month-old baby Peter went with me that night. It was so good to have them with me. In their presence, I was loved and wanted. My heart is at home!

Chapter Twenty

Return to Korea

In 1993, after several years of waitressing, substitute teaching, and math tutoring, I applied for and received a full-time math teaching job in the Souderton Area School District. I was told that, since I was a minority, I would be on the fast track to being hired. How ironic that my Amerasian features would now work to my advantage!

Several years into teaching full-time, our boys were finishing high school and going off to college. They both were football players and because of their age difference, they were able to play one year of both high school and college football together. Those were good times!

One of the few things that I knew about my birth father is that he was a lieutenant, an Army cook, and his name was "Shorty." My boys grew up hoping that his nickname was given to him because of a 6'5" stature. But at 5'9" and ready for college, they had long ago figured out that their grandfather was not very tall! The Fall of 2000 was one of those years where they were both playing football together at Lebanon Valley College, a Division III school. Doug had been a quarterback for many years, but due to a shoulder injury he became a senior wide receiver and Pete a freshman running back. We would go to every one of their Saturday games – after my husband finished his week as an assistant high school football coach.

One Friday afternoon that Fall, I received a phone call during a prep period at school. It led to one of the most meaningful experiences of my entire life.

It was the Director of Pearl S. Buck International. Their international office was now located at my former Green Hills Farm home just a few miles from our home. I was asked if I would go to Korea to

Football Days
with Dad and Uncles

Family
Scrapbook
Photos

present the Pearl S. Buck Woman of the Year Award to the South Korean President's wife, Madame Lee He Ho. Wow! But at that time, Pete was in the hospital with a football injury. I so appreciated the offer but said that, due to my son's illness, I would be unable to go. Then the director said something that took me some time to digest. "Julie, you can set the date to go. You can go anytime." Imagine that. Here we are talking about presenting a very prestigious award to a president's wife, and I get to pick the time we can go!

I knew this would be a wonderful experience, but I also knew what this would mean to the South Korean Amerasians like myself, born in the 1950's and '60's – we who were discriminated against, ridiculed, and not wanted by my mother land. Of course, this was my life. But, unlike so many, I was able to come to the land of my father's birth where a better life awaited me. And, Pearl S. Buck International represented my Mother Pearl who had made my journey to America possible. Now I had the opportunity to return to speak both on behalf of both the original Pearl S. Buck Foundation that had brought me to America in 1968 and on behalf of all the now adult Amerasian population with whom I spent my first fourteen years of poverty and rejection. What a privilege to also be asked to represent Pearl S. Buck International! "Will you be listening, Umma? Mother Pearl?"

The Koreans are very proud of their pure race and their orderly nation. We fatherless, nameless, shoeless Amerasians were misfits from the start. Far too many children were aborted by guilt-ridden mothers who feared for the future that their love child would face. My mother let me live. Now, thirty-three years after leaving Korea, one of those post-war Amerasians has been asked to set the date when she could go to Korea to present a Woman of the Year award to the South Korean President's wife. Only God could have orchestrated this! His grace certainly has a flair for the dramatic!

Our son recovered and was able to resume his studies at college and on January 12, 2001, my husband and I boarded a Korean Air Jet at JFK airport to head to Seoul. It was Doug's first trip to Korea and my first time back since I had come to America a third of a century before. What a mix of emotions I felt when, after a fifteen-hour flight, I touched Korean soil! My heart was pounding that I would soon see my mother's country where I had been born and raised in absolute poverty. I felt the joy of my mother's love, the pain of rejection by some and yet, the goodness of people abounded everywhere. Thank God that Doug was with me to share in my excitement, joys and fears. I had come back to the land that I so loved.

Carrying our suitcases and holding hands, we looked for Mr. Seung M. Kim, the Korean Director of Pearl S. Buck International in Sosa. However, he was not there, no greeting sign welcomed us. It was no use paging Mr. Kim because half of the airport would have responded to such a request! Evidently, he was caught in a traffic jam. When Mr. Kim finally arrived, we witnessed firsthand that traffic in Seoul is horrendous. As soon as we were on the road, we saw a bus ram the back of a fancy Korean car. Mr. Kim smiled and said, "Oh, he kissed him!" Thirty-three years ago, there was only one bridge crossing the Han River running through Seoul. In 2001, there were more than twenty.

We were treated like royalty by Mr. Kim and his assistant, Mr. Lee. Transportation and a daily schedule, including sight-seeing and meals, were efficiently provided for us. They were kind, gracious, and friendly men. One thing that impressed us was how quickly people walked to get from one place to another – and the disregard they seem to have when they bumped into others, including us. I finally asked Mr. Kim why some people do not say, "Excuse me," as they so quickly navigated the human traffic flow on the sidewalks. He thought a moment and said, "If people stopped to say excuse me every time, they bumped into someone, they would never get anywhere." That's how crowded downtown Seoul is.

With my speech prepared, we drove up to the Blue House. Americans have their White House but South Koreans have their Blue House. The guard met us and almost did not let us in with our video camera. We had promised our sons and our students at school that they would get some video to see from the visit. Then, a high-ranking official came out and said we could do limited video footage of this wonderful experience. When we were finally allowed in, we were treated as royalty, beyond our wildest expectations.

We had a nine-course dinner, foods that I had never had when I lived in Korea in the 1960's since we were so poor. Many Korean dignitaries were there, as well as a few officers representing our Armed

Seated from left: Julie's husband Doug Henning, the author Peter Conn, President Kim, his wife Madame Lee He Ho & Julie Henning.

Madame Lee He Ho & Julie Henning

Forces. The Blue House Palace was absolutely beautiful and majestic. The First Lady, Madame Le He Ho, was so very kind and gracious. I shared with them about my Korean memories – my Umma, our poverty, her death, the Pearl Buck Foundation, Mother Pearl, my education and my family. Would you believe she held my hand the whole time while we took many pictures? It was an absolutely exhilarating day! Both my Umma and Mother Pearl would have been so happy and proud that I was given this great honor!

The next morning, Tuesday, I remember saying to my husband, "You know, Sweetheart, we had such a great time yesterday. But, when the Lord isn't at the center of it, it somehow seems empty." Tuesday was going to be a quiet day compared to Monday's formalities. Little did we know what surprise God had in store for us.

We went to visit the Holt Adoption Agency as a courtesy visit, since Pearl S. Buck International partnered with the Holt Agency to bring hope to more orphaned or abandoned children worldwide. The Holt Adoption Agency was begun in 1955 by a compassionate American couple, Harry and Bertha Holt, who adopted eight Korean children to join the six that he and his wife already had. One of his six biological children, Molly, was now in her late-sixties and the Assistant Director of Holt.

Molly held this position primarily because in Korea, men were the directors of everything – whether they knew what they were doing or not! We saw very quickly that Molly was very capable her position as an assistant. Moreover, she had a passion and a purpose about her work. Molly told us, "Business had been my father's master, and we had lots of money. When the Lord became my father's master and we moved to Korea, we had purpose."

For almost fifty years, the Holt Agency was alive with activity, sending many Korean babies to eagerly awaiting American families for adoption. During our conversation with Molly, I mentioned that I remembered a time my mother dropped me off at a place to be adopted. Strangely, Molly asked, "Did she take you back?" to which I replied, "Yes, how did you know?" I had described the place where my mother had left me as having a flat roof at the end of a winding road up a hill. The entrance had a big iron gate.

Miss Holt told me that my description sounded like the former home for the children before Holt moved to its current location. She asked me to write my Korean name and birth date. Then, Molly asked, "Did your mother take her own life?" This was the second time in five minutes that Molly had seemingly read my mind. "Yes," I said, "when I was 13, my mother took her life a few months after safely dropping me off at the Pearl S. Buck Opportunity Center in Sosa, where she was assured that I'd be taken care of by an American family while attending the Pearl S. Buck Opportunity Center."

This woman, whom I had just met, who had devoted her lifetime working with Korean children and their mothers, seemed to know my past. I thought, "How many other Amerasians had lived through similar circumstances as me?" My story wasn't that different from the stories of many other Amerasians. Yet God chose to give me the hope of a new future in America.

Later that day, we visited with the Mayor of Bucheon City on the outskirts of Seoul. This was the chosen location for a future Pearl S. Buck Memorial site. I had lived as Pearl S. Buck's daughter for almost five years in my middle and late teens and now the Korean government was in the planning stages of honoring Mother Pearl's work in a nation that she loved dearly. After much planning and another grand, multi-course banquet and speeches, I gave some of my belongings from Mother Pearl to be displayed in her new museum. Among them was the suitcase which said "PSB," and the pearl hair pin that Mother used to wear but had given to me. This same suitcase that I had packed to go to Palmer House School in 1971 was used on my return trip to Korea in 2001. Now, having donated it to the museum, Doug and I had to purchase another suitcase to get our things back to America.

Later that evening when we returned to our Presidential Hotel in downtown Seoul, we found an envelope placed beneath the door of our room on the 27th floor. When we opened it, we saw that it had been delivered on behalf of Molly Holt. As we unfolded the paper, we were amazed to see that she had photocopied a record of my time at the Holt Adoption Agency when I was four years old! Included on the record was a picture of me. I had never seen a picture of myself any younger than eleven years old, so this was very special to my husband and me.

And, this paper describes me as a "white girl." On the upper left corner of the paper there was an address of a couple in northwest Pennsylvania, who were preparing to adopt me. I had always thought my Umma was quite old when she died. But this record, dated 1957, shows that she was only 26 at the time. This meant that when she died in 1967, she was only 36. Oh, how young she was! How much she loved me!

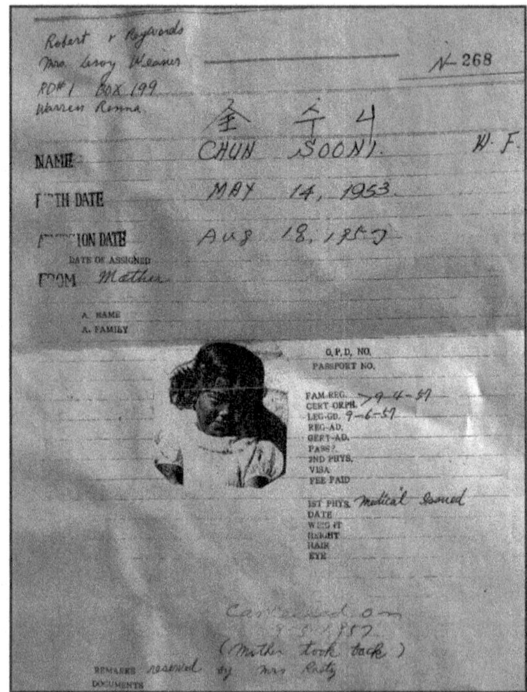
N-268

NAME CHUN SOONI W. F.

MAY 14, 1953

Aug 18, 1957

FROM Mother

O.P.D. NO.
PASSPORT NO.
FAM-REG. 9-4-57
CERT-ORPH.
LEG-GD. 9-6-57
REG-AD.
CERT-AD.
PASS?
2ND PHYS.
VISA
FEE PAID
1ST PHYS. Medical Issued
DATE
WEIGHT
HEIGHT
HAIR
EYE

(Mother took back)

REMARKS
DOCUMENTS

Holt Adoption Agency record of Julie

UNCONDITIONAL RELEASE

On this 18th Day of August, 1957, I Chong Song Cha, born 28 September 1930, #280 Pubwoni Chon Hyon Myon Paju Gun Kyongi, Korea, the legal custodian of a white girl Sooni, born 14 May 1953, father unknown, do hereby release all rights which I have as legal custodian of said child, and surrender the child to World Vision, Inc., Seoul, Korea.

Polio 5-22-57 (1st)

WITNESSES:

EARL F. MC NAYR
Chaplain(Capt)USA
24th DivArty

PFC Richard Jones
Chaplain's Assistent
24th DivArty

The next day, we visited a woman who had been my mother's best friend, Aunt Sughil, one of my Aunties. How good it was to see her after 33 years. She told us that my mother had given me up to be adopted at least twice – because she knew she was not able to adequately provide for me in the present, and that the future for me was bleak.

Each time I was away from her, Umma would cry and cry when she returned home to an empty house. Separation was more than she could bear and she came back to "kidnap" me from the orphanage. The Holt record also noted that my Umma took me back home with her after only 18 days with them. As a mother now myself, I can't even begin to measure the utter distress and agony that would compel a mother to give her child away.

Aunt Sughil, my Umma's best friend

Aunt Sughil said that my mother had no purpose for living without me! That explained much to me. My mother took her life after I went to the Pearl Buck Foundation in Sosa. What she did was not right, but I believe she did it for me. She loved me very much and she couldn't live without me, but she wanted what was best for me. Likely she thought, she couldn't let me go when I was little and, now that I was older, who else would want an older child? My mother knew I was safe at PSBI and that I had a future. Her job was finished.

Miss Holt told us that many mothers took their lives at that time. Perhaps they resorted to this because of the great love they had for their children, guilt for bringing them into a hostile world, and the hope to give their children better lives. I learned many years later, that in the Korean culture, it is a demonstration of heroic courage to give one's life for another. My Umma did that with my best in mind. I only wish she had not made that choice. I miss her so!

All these years, I could not bring myself to tell others besides my husband the truth about how my mother died. But, since I have been back to Korea, I have come to the realization that to withhold this truth from my story would be keeping back the fullness of all that God has allowed in my life. If we had gone to Korea as tourists, we would have never visited the Holt Adoption Agency. I never knew the name of Holt, and we would not have known some of my past. But God scheduled all of this in a very special way, and He wanted us to know from what past He had delivered me.

Having my husband with me in Korea was such a joy! He was able to see some of the places I would always tell him about. He even got to see the alley. When my husband saw this alley, his eyes were filled with tears. Six or seven other ladies had lived near me and were like my aunties. I was the only child around. They used to call me "the rose in the ditch." Reflecting on this, I believe I now know why I was the only child living with my mother. She chose life and she chose me.

The edge of the alley

I used to wonder why I was born in Pusan, the Southernmost part of the Korean Peninsula? When we visited Korea, we learned that the Chinese Army had forced the South Koreans and American soldiers to retreat south. That is most likely where my mother met my father. But my memory is only of living near the 38th parallel, the demilitarized zone, where the most concentrated location of U.S. Army bases were strategically situated.

One more interesting fact was revealed on my record from the Holt Adoption Agency. I found out that I was one year older than I had thought. I had always been told that I was born on May 14, 1954. But, my record from Holt clearly states: "Birth Date: May 14, 1953." So, we traveled thirteen time zones to find out that I was a year older than I thought I was. What a bummer!

After a glorious week of multiple and clear demonstrations of God's grace in my life, it was time for us to go home. We so appreciated the prayers of family and friends while we were on this journey. My trip was completely paid for by the Pearl S. Buck International. But the people at PSBI knew that I would not be going unless my husband went, too. So, it was decided that Doug's way could be paid for also, if we agreed to escort a Korean orphan from the Holt Agency to the baby's new adoptive parents, who would be eagerly awaiting our arrival at JFK Airport. We jumped at the idea! Who wouldn't want to bring a bundle of joy to excited new parents?

On our way to the airport, we stopped at Holt to pick up our six-month-old escort baby, Gabrielle. She was as cute as a button with her blue diaper bag, and we learned that her new parents lived just outside of Allentown, PA, less than an hour from our home!

Before we left Holt, we saw six other blue diaper bags of babies set to be delivered that day to locations all over the United States. Destinations included Seattle, Minneapolis, and Los Angeles. While we were still at Holt, we saw caregivers praying for the children. Then, they also asked to pray with us before we left with our Allentown-bound bundle. How moving! Later that day, they would be praying for the other babies that would go with the six blue diaper bags destined for eagerly awaiting parents at other U. S. airports. Baby Gabrielle was such a good traveler, smiling, eating, cooing and sleeping. Her new parents were so beyond blessed by Gabrielle and they adopted another little Korean girl named after me, Julia – and we still keep in touch!

My husband turned to me and said, "Sweetheart, when you were at the Holt Children's Home, you were being prayed for, too." The people who prayed for me when I was four did not know that I would come to know Christ as my Savior but God heard their prayers so many years ago and answered them – exceedingly, abundantly beyond!

Someday, I will see these faithful Holt caregivers in heaven and thank them. What a reminder for each of us to pray for our family, friends, loved ones, co-workers, neighbors, and others who do not yet know Jesus and the power of the Gospel. We don't know when God will answer, but He is gracious and will answer in His time.

Julie visiting her junior high school
in Korea in 2001

Chapter Twenty-One

Home

This is my story. This is His Story! God had a plan and a purpose for me even when I didn't know it. He allowed me to be born into a new, misunderstood race. When many Amerasians were aborted, He protected me. Through many years of ridicule, He gave me a loving mom who always wanted what was best for me.

He gave me a work ethic to study hard. This led Miss Buck to discover me and ultimately, my grades became my ticket to America. Mother Pearl's love and care gave me a second chance at life.

My adopted parents, Umma and Oppa Price, gave me love and security. They demonstrated how to live by and in faith. Now, I am blessed with a loving and giving husband, two wonderful sons and their loving wives, two lovely daughters-of-my-heart, five of the most amazing, adorable grandsons, with an extended family, friends, and Jesus!

You have a story to tell, too. God has a purpose and a plan to work out His best in each precious life He has made. As a math teacher, I learned that the 16th century mathematician Galileo wrote, "Mathematics is the alphabet in which God has written the universe."

When one considers the sunrise and sunset, the high and low tides, the eclipses, mathematicians can predict the next occurrence well in advance. As Galileo said about the universe – we are God's alphabet - God also faithfully writes the story of redemption in each of His children. In God's time and in His way, He brings His children to Himself. And, He chooses to use His children to make that redemptive story known to others.

The Bible says, "For all things work together for good to those who love God and are called according to His purpose." Not all things are good individually, but all things work together for good.

When I bake my favorite Pennsylvania Dutch "Funny Cake Pie," I put two cups of flour – I would not eat that flour alone; two cups of sugar – sugar is so sweet, but two cups are way too much to eat! Baking soda – yuk! Vanilla has such a sweet aroma, but is bitter to the taste. Then there is salt, oil, and cocoa. Many of these ingredients are not palatable alone, but when they are all mixed together and go through the heat, at just the perfect time in the oven…Voila!!! Out comes the most delicious cake.

All things are not good individually, but all things work together for good. The prophet Jeremiah writes to a people destined for a period of bondage under the rule of other nations, "For I know the plans I have for you, plans for your welfare, not for calamity, but to give you a future and a hope." I have a future. I have a hope. I have found Home!

Epilogue

In 2016, Sooni Goo Julie Comfort Walsh Price Henning retired as a middle-school math teacher after 25 years in the Souderton Area School District. For fourteen of those years, she taught on the same team as Doug, who left teaching in 2009 to become a full-time family care pastor at the church they have attended since they started dating almost five decades ago.

Julie left a lasting impression on her students as a knowledgeable, creative, passionate, caring, child-centered educator. Julie put the same energy into excelling in her chosen profession as she did keeping herself up late at night to study as a seventh-grader in a Sosa, South Korea dormitory. Julie works hard at each endeavor she pursues.

While teaching in a public school, Julie and her husband Doug facilitated a student-led bible study every Friday morning for close to 20 years. Julie, with her team of teachers as chaperones, would take around 150 middle school students on field trip each year to her Mother's home at Green Hills Farm. Her students would make handmade Christmas ornaments and decorate many Christmas trees for the new National Historic Landmark Home's annual Festival of Trees. Julie always felt that Mother's humanitarian work should be as famous as her writing career, and should be taught to the students and others. If not, if we chose to do nothing, Mother's legacy would be one generation from extinction.

By God's grace, Julie lives by a saying that has been close to her heart since the day she heard it many years ago, "Bloom where you are planted." God has had his hand of protection and blessing on her since her birth as an unwanted Amerasian in Pusan, South Korea in 1953. She and her mother were ostracized, but survived and their relationship thrived amidst abject poverty, a true "rose in a ditch." Julie's work ethic got Pearl S. Buck's attention. She was a "Comfort" to the Nobel Prize winning author until her death, and was then adopted and led to a relationship with Christ by Christian parents. She bloomed as a growing believer in their home while going to college and dating Doug. Her flower as a wife for over forty years has given off beauty and a sweet aroma even though times have sometimes been difficult. Some chronic health issues have resulted from her second pregnancy when Julie lost twins. She blooms anyway.

Julie continues to bloom as a mother and grandmother. Her two sons and her "daughters-in-love," Kandece and Renee, are a joy to her as well as five grandsons – Tre, Cole, Carter, Mason & Cade – the "fabulous five" ages seven to thirteen at this writing. Mom-Mom is so special to each of them, and they to her.

Sons Doug and Pete are successful in their professions, demonstrating character and integrity – one in education, the other in business. They are great husbands and dads, also. Their wives are loving moms and wonderful home managers who find the time to work part-time and help their homes thrive.

By the end of 2017, the entire family has individually trusted Jesus as Savior. All eleven belong to God's eternal family! As a child, Julie prayed to a God she did not yet know and asked for a family. Not only has God blessed her with the most wonderful immediate family of eleven, but He has also given Julie a wonderful extended family that loves to spend time together, and a church family that lives out Christian charity and care.

As a pastor's wife, Julie's perpetual smile, energy, words of encouragement/counsel, servant heart, and hospitality talents help others to bloom where they are, too. As so many others have invested in Julie, she, by God's grace, gives herself to others as well.

Julie has shared her story in nearly 300 churches and civic organizations. She blooms for God each time and shares how God, by His grace, used Pearl S. Buck and so many others to invest in her and bring her to a place where she found a home in America, a relationship with Christ and a family. God has given Julie the gift of evangelism to lovingly share the gospel with these ladies' groups.

Burdened for the cause of Amerasian children throughout Southeast Asia, Julie has participated in television programs, radio interviews, and newspaper articles. She has spoken numerous times at PSBI and appeared on television programs shown in South Korea and China.

Doug and Julie Henning 2019

Doug & Kandece's Wedding Day
L to R: Diane, Ray, Harry, Jean, Kandece, Doug, Julie, Pete & Doug

Pete & Renee's Wedding Day
L to R:
Kandece, Doug,
Renee, Pete,
Doug & Julie

Harry Price,
Julie Henning
& Jean Price

The Henning Family - L to R: back row,
Renee, Pete, Doug, Julie, Doug, Kandece holding Cade,
front row, Mason, Carter, Tre & Cole

Adults: Kandece, Doug, Julie, Doug, Pete, Renee
Children: Tre, Cole, Cade, Carter & Mason

The Fabulous Five
aka "The Fab Five"
back row
Cole, Doug, Julie & Tre
front row
Mason, Cade & Carter

"The Fab Five"
stacked top to bottom
Cade, Mason, Carter
Cole & Tre

Backyard play with the boys

Mom-Mom's
special collage
painting depicting
"The Fab Five"
as five little fish
following her.

Julie with her daughters-in-love Renee & Kandece

Pictures taken on a recent cruise.

Julie with her sons Pete & Doug

She has also spoken in elementary, middle, and high school groups, a local university as well as at the Rogers & Hammerstein Homestead. Julie has also had the honor to take part in presenting the "Pearl S. Buck International Woman of the Year Award" to then First Lady, Laura Bush, in 2006.

In 2018, Pearl S. Buck International's Korean office in Bucheon City, South Korea, asked Julie to be the keynote speaker at their first Pearl S. Buck Legacy Symposium. While Julie was not able to attend personally, she was grateful that the organizers of the symposium offered her the opportunity to send them a seven-minute greeting from her home in Pennsylvania.

In her brief message, she was prompted to mention the name of her mother, Jung Song Ja, and the treasured, unfathomable influence she had in Julie's life. This video was watched by South Korean dignitaries and scholars. Before them, Julie's voice proclaimed the name of a woman of no reputation, who never had more than a grade school education, but whose love and sacrifice gave Julie the foundation upon which God has so patiently and lovingly constructed her life. Perhaps that name had not been uttered in South Korea since her death over a half-century ago. But the name 'Jung Song Ja' was heard by some of South Korea's finest on October 30, 2018.

Julie accompanying the former First Lady Laura Bush in 2006, that year's recipient of the Pearl S. Buck Woman of the Year award on a guided tour of Pearl's historic Green Hills Farm.

Personalized photo portrait of Laura Bush and Julie Henning in front of the famous Pearl portrait in the Cultural Center

Julie Henning speaking recently at the Rogers & Hammerstein homestead. Both men were friends of Pearl S. Buck.

MyHeritage DNA

Europe	50.2%
North and West Europe	40.2%
Scandinavian	22.9%
Irish, Scottish, and Welsh	7.2%
North and West European	6.9%
Finnish	3.2%
East Europe	5.9%
East European	5.9%
Ashkenazi Jewish	4.1%
Ashkenazi Jewish	4.1%
Asia	49.8%
Julie Henning	100.0%

My Heritage DNA Report - So many connections in a story that is still unfolding!

Also in 2018, a dear friend gave Julie a DNA kit for her birthday and said, "It's about time you found out something about your father." In recent months, Julie and Doug have identified her father. He passed away a few years ago. Will Julie ever meet her half-siblings? Do they know she exists? Did her father, most likely not Shorty Lieutenant, even know she existed? That's all part of the story God is still writing.

Several years ago, Julie and Doug made their first and only trip to Grand Canyon Country in Arizona. While hiking in a field of volcanic ash near Flagstaff, Julie stopped in her tracks when she saw one bright orange flower apparently thriving in the hard, barren land. With a tear on her cheek, Julie said to her husband, "Out of the ashes is this beauty. How good God is! He put this flower here to remind me of how He wants me to reflect His strength, love, and grace wherever I am."

Realize that your home is where you are and who is with you. Find your home, thank God for it, and bloom!

A rose can thrive – even in a ditch.

– Doug Henning

Special Exhibit

Please Be Our Guest
as we celebrate the opening of
a special exhibit presented by
Bucheon City, Gyeonggi Province, South Korea

Lasting Relationships & Meaningful Impact
of
Pearl Buck & the Korean People

Saturday, October 5, 2019
1–4 pm
Pearl S. Buck International
520 Dublin Road, Perkasie, PA 18944

Light Refreshments
Pearl S. Buck House Station Tours

Official Ceremony
marking the beginning of cultural exchange between
Pearl S. Buck International and Bucheon City, Korea
Korean Entertainment / Children's Activities
Ribbon Cutting
Exhibit Tour

Kindly register on or before
Friday, September 13 at
www.pearlsbuck.org/celebrate
for each person attending

Bridging Cultures - Changing Lives

Ribbon cutting ceremony at the Pearl S. Buck Welcome Center for the opening of a special exhibit presented by Bucheon City, South Korea and Pearl S. Buck International of America (October 5, 2019) L to R, Julie Henning, Mr. Hyo-joon Cho (Director of Culture & Economy of Bucheon),Mr. Young-gwang Jeong (President of Bucheon Culture Center) Janet Mintzer (CEO of PSBI) & Mr. Eui-yeol Choi (Executive Director of Bucheon Culture Center)

PSBI's display featuring photo highlights of Julie Henning's personal story, many of which appear in this book.

Doug, Julie and Hyo-joon Cho Director of Culture & Economy of Bucheon City, South Korea who presented a framed caricature of Julie to her at the tent reception.

Doug and Julie greeting guests at the special exhibit, displaying the framed caricature Julie had been gifted.

Janet Mintzer, at left, on stage as Julie Henning, on right, addresses the guests of the Special Exhibit.

The Sosa Opportunity Center exhibit featured Julie's 2018 video address recorded for Bucheon City's first Pearl S. Buck Legacy Symposium. Though Julie wasn't able to attend the symposium in person, organizers offered her the opportunity to send them a seven-minute greeting from her home in Pennsylvania.

Sooni Goo Julie Comfort Walsh Price Henning

Made in USA - North Chelmsford, MA
1223210_9781704786438
02.28.2022 1401